MW01155778

STICKLINKS
AND TRICKLEDOWNS

By Terry Stickels

imagine!
Publishing
New York
www.imaginebks.com

Library of Congress Cataloging-in-Publication Data

Stickels, Terry H.
 Go games! trickledowns & sticklinks / Terry Stickels, Tony
 Immanuvel.
     p. cm.
 ISBN 978-1-936140-11-4 (pbk. : alk. paper)
 1. Puzzles. I. Immanuvel, Tony. II. Title.
 GV1493.S8235 2010
 793.73--dc22

                              2010001403
10 9 8 7 6 5 4 3 2 1

Published by Imagine Publishing, Inc.
25 Whitman Road, Morganville, NJ 07751

Printed in China
Manufactured in July 2010

ISBN 13: 978-1-936140-11-4

For information about custom editions, special sales, premium and
corporate purchases, please contact Imagine Publishing, Inc. at
specialsales@imaginebks.com

INTRODUCTION

When *USA WEEKEND* magazine first decided to run *TRICKLEDOWNS* on their Web site over ten years ago, the response from readers was immediate and pleasantly surprising. Would the magazine run more of these and was there a book available? Several years later I had the pleasure of introducing *StickLinks* in the magazine, and the response was the same. The magazine has continued to feature both puzzles throughout the years and now, for the first time, they appear together in this book.

What makes these puzzles so popular and fun? In the case of *TRICKLEDOWNS*, they had a good track record before my version appeared. Lewis Carroll, of *Alice's Adventures in Wonderland* fame (whose real name was Charles Dodgson), created a version called "doublets" in 1879 that were published in *Vanity Fair* magazine. They were an immediate hit and versions of them have been around ever since. Here is how Carroll described the puzzles:

"The rules of the Puzzle are simple enough. Two words are proposed, of the same length; and the Puzzle consists in linking these together by interposing other words, each of which shall differ from the next word in one letter only. That is to say, one letter may be changed in one of the given words, then one letter in the word so obtained, and so on, till we arrive at the other given word. The letters must not be interchanged among themselves, but each must keep to its own place. As an example, the word 'head''may be changed into 'tail' by interposing the words 'heal, teal, tell, tall.' I call the given words 'a Doublet,' the interposed words 'Links,' and the entire series 'a Chain,' of which I here append an example:

H	E	A	D
h	e	a	l
t	e	a	l
t	e	l	l
t	a	l	l
T	A	L	L

TRICKLEDOWNS are slightly different in that you are required to change one letter at a time, but once that letter has been changed, it must remain that letter throughout. Because of this, if you start with a five-letter word, you will have five steps or "ladders" to complete to arrive at the new word—and all five letters will be different from what they were at the beginning of the puzzle. You will find four-, five-, and six-letter TRICKLEDOWNS in this book—196 of them. If you are anything like the other people who play these puzzles, you will find yourself carrying this book around with you to solve a puzzle wherever and whenever you have the chance.

StickLinks are puzzles I created along with my friend and fellow puzzle designer Tony Immanuvel. These are original word puzzles that combine two popular puzzles: Word Search and guessing famous quotes. The rules are simple but the puzzles range from easy to challenging depending upon the length of the quote. Each puzzle starts off by giving you the first letter of the quote found in a grid of letters. Your job is to link the letters together by drawing lines from one letter to the next until you eventually come up with a famous quote—and usually a humorous one, at that. Like *TRICKLEDOWNS*, *StickLinks* have an addictive quality to them. Not only is it fun to have created a puzzle no one else makes, but I have just as much fun finding great quotes and creating the puzzles as the solvers do finding their solutions. I receive letters from readers aged nine to nineth-nine asking for books of these so they can have ready access any time of the day. Here is the first of what I hope will be many more.

This is one of the best times in history to be a puzzle writer. It seems people enjoy puzzles now more than ever. They're fun, challenging, inexpensive, and rewaring when you finally reach that AHA! moment of victory over the solution. One of the reasons it's the best of times for me is because of you, the puzzle solvers. Your letters to me are full of bright, clever ideas and approaches for all kinds of puzzles. Every day brings some new, refreshing idea. It also doesn't hurt that scientists have found that solving puzzles and games are two of the best portals for keeping your mind flexible and possibly even staving off some forms of age-related dementia.

It isn't often that someone has the pleasure of combining their avocation with their vocation. I'm one of those lucky few. I can honestly say that at some point every day I laugh hysterically at the innovative, creative, silly things I see in Puzzleland, as well as the great letters I receive from puzzle fans. I want that to continue for as long as I can have that happen. Send me a note or a letter and let me know what you think of the puzzles in this book. I would enjoy hearing from you and I promise you'll get a response. You can reach me at www.terrystickels.com

Have fun and spread the word: Puzzles will make you rich, beautiful, and anything else you would like to be . . . well, maybe that's being a little bold, but like I said, there are lots of silly things in Puzzleland!

Terry Stickels
January 15, 2010

StickLinks are puzzles that combine quotes with word searches. A quote is placed in a grid and the solver must connect the letters of the quote with a continuous line. For example, to find the hidden phrase in the puzzle below, start with the circled letter. Next, draw a line from each correct letter to the next as you reveal the phrase. The blanks at the bottom will also help. When the puzzle is done, each letter will have been used only once, and the letters will be connected with a straight line.

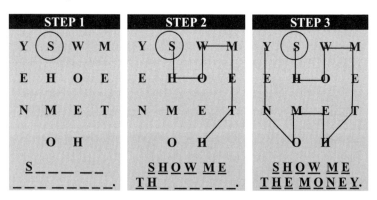

1

```
S   T   H   E   R
K   I   I   S   E
C   L       D   U
G   U   E   O   E
N   I   S   D   F
```

____ __ ___ _____
__ _____.

Branch Rickey

2

```
M   R   E   Y   W
P   A   K   C   A
A   E   E   R   L
Y   M   I   M   A
B   E   C   O   E
```

____ _____ ___,
_____ _ _____.

Will Rogers

3

```
G  A  S  E  I  F
E  R  Y  I  L  O
E  R  O     S  T
D  T  S  I  A  E
U  P  O  N (H) S
```

_ _ _ _ _ _ _ _ _ _ _ _ _   _ _

_ _ _ _ _ _ _ _ _ _ _ _ _ _.

Napoleon Bonaparte

4

```
   (F) L  T  E
   E  L  O  U  T  R
   E  I  T  A  B  F
   B  A  K  E  A  L
   E  I  G  T  S  Y
      K  L  N  I
```

_ _ _ _ _ _ _ _ _ _

_ _ _ _ _ _ _ _, _ _ _ _ _

_ _ _ _ _ _ _ _.

Muhammad Ali

5

```
    B   E   N   A
T   G   E   I   T   C
H   R   U   A   S   T
G   H   V   O   Y   A
U   A   N   E   B   E
O   H   T   I   N   E
```

— —   — — — — —   — —   — — —,   — —

— — —   — — — —   — — — —   — —

— — — — — — —.

William Shakespeare

6

```
D   T   A   H   W   N
O   S   A   S   T   O
I   E   N   T   N   E
T   T   I       A   O
C   B   S   F   S   I
H   A   E   M   Y   H
```

—   — — — —   — —   — — — — — —

— — — —,   — —   — — — —

— — — — —   — — — —.

Gilda Radner

7

```
    L  E  S  I  R  A
(T) F  T  H  T  N  S  E
 H  E  L  Y  I  G  I  F
 O  N  A  H  E  W  E  R
    V  E  T  O  F  A
```

— — —   — — — —   — — — — —   — —

— — — —   — —   — — — —   — —

— — — —   — — — — — —.

Franklin D. Roosevelt

8

```
(A) N  I  B  D  R
 K  N  D  Y  L  F  L  O
 E  A  E  Y  E  A  O  W
 S  M  E  E  N  R  L  E
    T  H  E  W  H  O
```

— —   — — —   — — —   — —   — — —

— — — —   — — —   — — — —

— — — —   — — — — —.

Mahatma Gandhi

9

```
    O   U   N   I   R
Y   F   D   O   W   O   N
D   I  (Y)  Y   O   O   I
E   L   O   U   R   A   N
I   P   S   U   C   N   G
    O   T   E   G   T
```

— — — — — — —   , — — —

— — — — — —   — —   — — —   — —

— — — —   — — —   — — — — — —.

Meryl Streep

10

```
    F   D   A   T   S
R   O   N   I   N   H   O
O   N   H  (T)  O   G   W
I   T   T   H   S   E   R
N   H   F   Y   N   A   O
```

— — — —   — — —   — — — —   — — —

— — — — — —   — — — —   — — —

— — — — — — —.

Alexander Hamilton

11

```
    A  T  I  O  N
 C  D  E  F  O  S  I
(T) U  E  H  T  T  L
 E  H  I  L  U  O  E
 S  H  G  E  S  A  R
    T  R  E  C  N
```

___ _____ _____
__ _____ __
_____.

Helen Keller

12

```
    E  M  E  I  E
 S  S  T  A  N  S  U
 P  I  S  I  F  I  A
 N  T  M  E  H  S  C
 A  R  O (I) T  T  H
    C  H  N  G  O
```

__ _____ __ ___
_____, _____ _ ____
__ _____.

Popeye

13

```
M  T  A  D  M  A  T  S
E  O  S  A (Y) Y  A  T
W  O  E  S     O  C  N
H  E  N  K  Y  U  U  G
O  M  A  O  U  L  A  H
```

___ ____ ____ ___

__ _____ ___

_____ ___ _____.

Jay Leno

14

```
I  S  M  R  E  A  N  T
N  I  T  O  M  I  T  T
(I) O  A  E     P  R  H
M  N  I  G  O  N  O  A
A  G  D  E  L  W  K  N
```

_____ __ ____

_____ ____

_____.

Albert Einstein

15

```
    H   A   S   H   E   A
R   M   A   F   T   O   R
E   O   N   T   I   N   D
H   U   U   L   R   E   O
T   S   M   U  (Y)  F   Y
O   M   Y   O   U   O
```

_ _ _ _ ,   _ _ _   _ _ _ _ _ _

_ _ _ _   _ _   _ _ _ _ _ _   _ _ _

_ _ _ _ _   _ _   _ _ _ .

Jay Leno

16

```
   (I)  A   V   E   E   N
E   Y   F   H   T   M   E
C   V   O   U   N   O   I
H   R   A   H   D   S   E
R   A   A   T   D   Y   O
E   T   C   N   O   U
```

_ _   _ _ _   _ _ _ _   _ _ _ _

_ _ _ _ _ _ ,   _ _ _   _ _ _ _ ,

_ _ _ _   _ _ _ _ _ _ _ .

Paul Newman

17

```
    I   R   E   M   A   E
C   S   O   D   A   H   T
A   S   D   I   R   T   U
N   O   B   Y   L   E   O
M   D   R  (K)  M   I   E
A   E   I   L   L   V
```

_ _ _ _   _ _   _ _ _ _?   _ _   _

_ _ _ _   _ _ _ _   _ _ _   _ _ _

_ _ _ _ _ _ _   _ _ _ _ _?

Homer Simpson

18

```
(O)  R   S   H   E   M   E
 R   O   T   A   E   W   N
 K   A   E   R   V   H   T
 A   I   E   M   O   T   E
 E   S   U   S   S   E   N
 W   A   C   R   I   H   T
```

_ _ _ _ _ _   _ _ _   _ _ _ _

_ _ _ _ _ _   _ _ _ _   _ _ _ _ _

_ _ _ _   _ _   _ _ _ _.

Cicero

19

```
A  P  E (M) I  F  I  L
O  R  R  A  E  S  E  L  L
F  T  S  S  N  K  T  F  U
T  H  E  O  E  A  S  O  F
E  D  U  P  A  Y  R  A
```

_ _ _ _ _ _   _ _ _   _ _ _ _

_ _   _ _ _   _ _ _ _   _ _ _

_ _ _ _   _ _ _   _   _ _ _ _

_ _ _ _.

Sophia Loren

20

```
O  H  I  K  L  U  O  C
N  U  T  L  T  D  Y  U (A)
J  I  T  I  L  I  F  O  S
U  N  W  E  M  E  N  I  Y
R  I  G  E  T  R  I  T
```

_ _   _ _   _ _ _   _ _ _ _ _

_ _ _   _ _ _ _   _ _ _ _ _ _

_ _ _ _ _ _ _   _ _ _ _ _ _ _ _.

Henry David Thoreau

21

```
F  E  R  E  D  D  I  B
I  V  M  W  T  A  H  E  T
R  E  V  E  N  S  N  G  S
T  E  T  A  H  H  D  H  I
U  O  W  I  T  T  H  E
```

— — — — — — — — — — — — — — — —
— — — — — — — — — — — —
— — — — — — — — — — — —.

George Washington

22

```
T  I  N  U  T  O  P  P
Y  E  M  I  D  D  R  S  O
H  F  I  Y  R  E  L  E  E
I  T  F  D  E  V  F  O  I
N  I  C  U  L  T  Y  L
```

— — — — — — — — — — — — —
— — — — — — — — — — — —
— — — — — — — — — — — — — — —.

Albert Einstein

23

```
   (F) E  A  N  E
  E  O  M  R  F  D  Q
  B  R  Y  F  O  Y  U
  L  T  O  R  X  T  A
  L  I  Y  I  R  A  L
  W  W  O  U  S  T  P
     E  S  R  E  N
```

_ _ _ _ _   _ _ _   _ _ _,   _ _ _ _ _

_ _ _   _ _.   _ _ _   _ _ _ _ _

_ _ _ _ _ _   _ _   _ _ _ _   _ _.

Joan Rivers

24

```
   (W) S  R  H  T
  O  T  H  A  E  O  T
  Y  N  E  N  T  O  O
  O  A  T  D  O  Y  D
  U  T  W  O  O  U  T
  R  O  N  F  D  O  O
     S  E  L  D  N
```

_ _ _ _   _ _ _   _ _   _ _ _

_ _ _ _   _ _ _ _   _ _

_ _ _ _ _ _ _,   _ _   _ _ _   _ _

_ _   _ _ _ _ _ _.

Confucius

25

```
 A  C  G  L  F  H  T  A
 A  H  I  N  I  I  E  N  G  E
 L  V  E  V  E  I  S  O  N  D
 E  N  I  U  Q  E  H  T  T  I
    T  O  F  A  V  O  I  D
```

_ _ _ _ _ _ _ _   _ _ _ _   _ _

_ _ _   _ _ _   _ _ _ _ _ _ _ _ _

_ _   _ _ _ _ _ _ _ _   _ _ _ _ _.

Ayn Rand

26

```
 C  O  C  A  R  E  D  T
 Y  W  R  U  S  I  E  B  D  O
 A  P  Y  A  G  N  S  A  E  A
 U  A  N  G  E  I  D  S  T  H
    G  N  I  L  D  T  U  B
```

_ _ _ _ _ _   _ _   _ _ _ _ _

_ _ _ _ _   _ _   _ _ _ _   _ _ _

_ _ _ _ _ _ _   _ _   _ _ _ _ _ _.

John Wayne

19

27

```
    E   I   L   R   S   I   F   Y
U   A   V   E   V   M   A   O   U   L
L   O   S   I   R   E   A   E  (D)  L
D   L   Y   F   D   O   F   R   L   I
    I   E   T   O   A   Y   E   V
```

_ _ _ _   _ _   _ _   _ _ _ _ _ ,

_ _ _ _   _ _ _ _ _ _ ,   _ _ _ _

_ _   _ _   _ _ _ _ _   _ _ _

_ _ _ _ _.

James Dean

28

```
    W   O  (I)  A   M   N   I   E
H   W   N   K   N   O   A   D   L   A
G   E   R   T   I   D   S   I   Y   A
O   M   I   E   B   T   I   M   Y   W
    I   N   G   U   T   O   N   M
```

_   _ _   _ _   _ _ _ _ _ _ _.   _

_ _ _   _ _ _   _ _ _ _   _ _

_ _ _ _   _ _ _   _ _   _ _   _ _

_ _ _.

Carl Sandburg

29

```
    M  C  A  T  E  D  I  S
 O  P  I  D  N  A  L  F  E  D
 C  Y  L  E  E  L  O  E  C  I
 L  S  D  N  P (G) S  P  T  V
    S  E  L  M  I  Y  L  E
```

_ _ _ _   _ _   _ _ _ _ _ _ _ _ _ _

_ _ _ _ _ _   _ _ _

_ _ _ _ _ _ _ _ _

_ _ _ _ _ _ _ _ _ _ _.

Arnold Palmer

30

```
    (A) Y  D  N  A  T
    N  M  N  A  I  E  I
    O  A  M  A  T  O  N
    E  S  N  B  U  M  S
    V  I  F  L  A  Y  R
    I  D  D  A  L  I  S
    L  A  E  N  A  E
```

_   _ _ _   _ _ _   _ _ _,

_ _ _ _ _ _ _   _ _ _   _ _ _ _

_ _ _   _ _ _ _,   _ _ _   _ _

_ _ _ _   _ _ _ _ _   _ _.

John F. Kennedy

31

```
    U   C   A   I   O   L   O   O
 (E) D   S   E   T   I   N   D   Y   T
    I   V   T   P   B   E   S   E   A   E
    S   O   R   O   H   T   E   G   O   N
    I   O   N   F   R   T   H   J   U   R
```

_ _ _ _ _ _ _ _   _ _   _ _ _

_ _ _ _   _ _ _ _ _ _ _ _   _ _ _

_ _ _   _ _ _ _ _ _   _ _   _ _ _

_ _ _.

Aristotle

32

```
    U   T   U   F   E   H   T   T   U   O
    R   E  (I)  M   A   L   L   Y   A   B
    T   T   T   O   K       A   E   S   E
    O   S   H   P   E   I   C   I   P   S
    U   G   R   E   D   I   C   T   O   N
```

,

_ _ _   _ _ _ _ _   _ _   _ _ _ _

_ _ _ _ _ _ _ _ _,

_ _ _ _ _ _ _ _   _ _ _ _ _

_ _ _   _ _ _ _ _ _.

Yogi Berra

33

```
E  S  Y  L  A  E  R  G  R  E
L  O  U  F  T  V  L  L  Y  F
P  E  I  F  I     I  A  G  F
P  V  R  R  E  R  A  E  R  U
L  A  I (T) T  T  M  E  N  S
```

_ _ _ _ _ _   _ _ _ _ _ _

_ _ _ _ _ _   _ _ _ _ _ _ _ _,

_ _ _ _ _   _ _ _   _ _ _ _ _

_ _ _ _ _ _ _.

Bertrand Russell

34

```
S  I  D  M  R  E  A  A  H (H)
E  O  A  I  L  L  U  S  E  D
C  F  E  H  T  V  T  E  I  I
I  H  T  N  E  A  I  R  S  S
V  E  O  N  D  N  E  K  I  L
```

_ _   _ _ _   _ _ _   _ _ _

_ _ _ _ _ _   _   _ _ _ _ _ _

_ _ _   _ _ _ _   _ _   _ _ _

_ _ _ _   _   _ _ _ _ _ _.

Sir Winston Churchill

35

```
E  B  E  H  T  (A) R  E  V
T  S  E  I  S  G  A  L  H  E  E
R  M  O  C  E  F  R  D  R  A  I
C  E  F  O  N  I  O  P  I  N  S
   I  P  E  R  H  A  P  E  S
```

— ———— ————— ——
—— ——— ————— ———
———————— — ————
———— ——.

Jane Austen

36

```
E  C  A  E  A  B  O  O
T  N  (B) R  H  A  L  H  K
I  F  E  G  I  D  E  T  S
R  U  L  A  N  O  R  O  Y
P  A  F  O  B  U  T  M  U
S  I  M  E  I  D  Y  A
```

—— —————— ————
—————— —————
————. ——— ——— ———
—— — ————————.

Mark Twain

37

```
    O  H  N  S  L  B  A  K
 S  N  C  I  A  A  E  T  N
 T  E  I  N  A  Q  I  E  I
 B  T  L  P  I  S  U  A  H
 R  U  I  O  D  O  U  S  T
 G  L  A  R  O  G (A) N
```

— ————— ———————————
—— ————— ——
—————————— —— ——
————— —————— .

H. L. Mencken

38

```
    D  C  T  I  O  A  R  Y
 A  S  I  E  H  W  N  H (T)
 I  K  R  C  E  E  C  N
 O  R  E  C  S  A  L  O  L
 W  E  S  U  S  S  C  P  Y
 R  O  F  E  B  E  M  O
```

——— ———— —————
———— —————— ————
————— ———— —— —
—————————— .

Vidal Sassoon

39

```
W  O  I  T  H  E  R  (I)
E  Y  U  N  E  A  R  U  F
R  O  T  N  T  R  P  O  Y
A  S  N  E  E  E  H  D  C
S  N  C  N  V  R  L  A  H
E  C  A  H  E  R  D  I
```

__ __   __ __ __ __   __ __ __ __ __ __

__ __ __ __ __   __ __ __   __ __ __ __ __ __ __,

__ __ __ __ __ __ __   __ __ __   __ __ __

__ __ __ __ ,   __ __ __ __ __ __.

Dick Cavett

40

```
E  V  O  H  T  T  A  H  V  (E) I
S  I  C  M  E  E  R  W  E  E  G
A  I  O  N  T     V  R  M  I  O
B  G  A  M  A  T  I  O  Y  T  T
O  U  T  M  S  T  I  E  M  A  O
```

__ __ __ __ __   __ __ __ __,   __   __ __   __ __

__   __ __ __ __,   __ __ __   __ __ __ __ __,

__ __   __ __ __ __ __   __ __ __ __   __ __ __

__ __ __ __ __ ,   __ __ __ __ __.

Steven Spielberg

41

```
      B   R   I   G   E
  H   N   E   L   D   U   S
  G   O   T   D   I   B  (W)
  U   O   T   A   N   E   W
  N   N   O   O   M   Y   A
      D   A   S   L   L
```

_ _   _ _ _ _ _   _ _ _   _ _ _ _

_ _ _ _ _   _ _ _   _ _ _

_ _ _ _ _   _ _ _ _ _ _ _.

Sir Isaac Newton

42

```
      S   N   I   O   T   S
      G   I   K   E   R   O
      H   A   S       E   O
      T   I   T   O   H   D
     (M)  S   P   E   N   T
```

_ _ _ _ _ _ _   _ _ _ _   _ _ _

_ _ _ _ _   _ _   _ _ _ _ _ _ _.

Terry Stickels

```
H  N  E  H  W  E  R  E  B  O  T
A  T  I  T  F  R  A  E  T  N  T
P  P  O (I) A     I  H  J  U  A
E  N  A  D  F  O  D  I  S  O  W
S  N  M  E  A  T  H  T  D  N  T
```

— —— —— —————— —— ,
————. — ———— ———
——— —— —— ————
——— —— ——————.

Woody Allen

43

```
E  S  A  H  T  L  A  E  W  Y  H
I  N  Y  T  O  B  E  D  S  L  T
W  D  L  Y  A     A  K  E  A  A
(E) R  Y  L  R  E  D  N  A  M  E
A  T  O  R  I  S  E  M  A  N  H
```

_ _ _ _ _ _ _ _ _ _ _ _
_ _ _ _ _ _ _ _ _ _ _ _ _ _
_ _ _ _ _ _ _ _ _ _ _,
_ _ _ _ _ _ _, _ _ _ _ _ _ _.

Benjamin Franklin

44

(B) S N E Y P L A N T H
A L E I T R E A N D E
A B L L N   C T T E O
C Y A I S I E N R M T
I S H P S F L A H E H

_ _ _ _ _ _   _ _   _ _ _ _ _
_ _ _ _ _ _   _ _ _ _ _   _ _ _
_ _ _   _ _ _ _   _ _ _ _   _ _
_ _ _ _ _ _ _ _.

Yogi Berra

45

```
Y  L  L  E  R  E  E  L  P  O  E
T  G  A  T  H  N  R  A  L  T  P
R  O  Y  R  I  I  G  E  E  I  A
A  O  D  E  E  T  B  S  V  E  H
E  H  T  A  V  E  I  P  E (D) T
```

_ _ _ _ _ _   _ _ _ _ _ _ _ _ _ ,

_   _ _ _ _ _ _   _ _ _ _

_ _ _ _ _   _ _ _   _ _ _ _ _ _

_ _ _   _ _   _ _ _ _ _.

Anne Frank

46

31

```
(T) H  E  I  S  K  N  I  N  S  O
 E  S  R  T  S  E  C  O  W  G  M
 N  O  E  C  O  S  C  H  T  E  G
 K  W  S  F  S  U  O  N  I  N  T
 E  S  L  E  Y  D  O  B  T  A  H
```

— — —   — — — — — —   — —

— — — — — —   — —   — — — — — —

— — — — — — — — —   — — — —

— — — — —   — — — —   — — — — —.

Aristotle Onassis

47

```
    O  E  P  S  T  P  E  C  C  A
  P  L  E  U  B  T  H  T  A  C  R  T
  M  E  L  L  A  O  A (I) N  T  E  O
  E  K  I  C  E  M  T  G  D  O  E  B
    A  S  M  B  E  R  S  N  O  L
```

— —————'— ———— ——

————— —— — ————

———— —————— ——————

———— —— —— ——————.

Groucho Marx

48

(E) E N A L N O C A Y
D N N G G U R O M I E B
A A A G A A O E M R S D
M D N L A C W T T I D E
 E R I C O U N V I D

_____   ___   _____

___   ___   _____

_____   __   _   _____

_____.

George Bernard Shaw

49

```
E  S  O  H  S  I  K  I  N  A
Ⓘ  M  A  U  E  K  E  H  E  M  A  E
R  A  M  O  U  S  R  E  P  E  I  V
V  A  L  U  O  V  E  E  P  E  L  A
E  S  H  E  R  Y  T  I  M  E
```

— —— — ————————

———————— —————

——— — ———— — ———

— ———— ——— —————.

Zsa Zsa Gabor

50

```
    E   Z   E   O   F   Y   O   K   W   I
(N) E   V   I   E   H   T   R   U   C   E   T
    R   O   N   U   S   E   Y   F   P   H   C   H
    C   E   L   F   S   O   E   O   A   Y   T   H
    T   N   A   T   R   U   Z   I   S   E
```

_____ _____ ___

____ __ ____

_____ ____ ___

____ __ ____ _____

Marlon Brando

51

```
    O   I   E   C   X   E   A   E   K   A
  N   N   E   T   P   E   N   O   U   C   A   M
 (I)  O   F   V   A   C   B   Y   R   E   S   O
  G   R   R   E   F   U   N   B   L   L   I   T
    E   T   A   T   I   E   G   L   A   D
```

—   — — — —   — — — — —   —
— — — ,   — — —   — —   — — —
— — — —   — — —   — —   — — —   — —
— — — —   — —   — — — — — — — —.

Groucho Marx

52

```
O  G (A) E  M  O  C  Y  E  H
T  S  L  R  T  N  E  T  W  T  S  I
O  Y  W  S  U  O  U  R  N  O  E  W
O  A  E  O  Y  O  L  F  A  L  T  R
T  H  R  P  E  P  E  S  S  O  H  E
```

_ _ _ _ _ _ ,   _ _   _ _   _ _ _ _ _

_ _ _ _ _ _   _ _ _ _ _ _ _ _ ,   ,

_ _ _ _ _ _ _ _ _   _ _ _ _   _ _ _ _

_ _ _ _   _ _   _ _ _ _ _ .

Yogi Berra

53

```
    F  U  A  L  O  O  H  O  H  W
 W  L  G  A  T  W  S  W  K  N (A) N
 I  S  E  H  T  E  O  B  O  P  S  O
 L  E  M  I  H  C  A  T  E  S  E  R
 L  N  V  E  R  S  E  A  M  U  E  D
```

_ _____ ___ _____
___ __ ____ __
_____ ____ ____
_____ __ __ _____.

Shirley MacLaine

54

```
T  E  Y  N  T  U  T  I  A  R  O  F
G  E  O  I  I  N  T  T  I  N  Y  D
A  S  I  T  E  S     I  S  N  N  A
I  A  A  A  R  I  T  U  T  M  O  E
R  R  Ⓜ  G  O  N  B  U  T  I  T  R
```

— — — — — — —   — —   —   — — — — —

— — — — — — — — — —,   — — —   — —'—

— — —   — — — — —   — — —   — —

— — — — — — — — — —   — — —.

Mae West

55

R S S I F W A N T E T H
O E D H (I) Y H T A H D E
H R A A E E T E P W E Y
E A S K I D P A O L U W
T S F D A S E V H D L O

__ _ ___ ____

_____ ___ ____

_____, ____ _____

____ ____ _____

_____.

Henry Ford

56

```
B  A  V  I  R  E  O  H  T  O  B
O  E  S  I  P  P  E  L  P  A  S  E  S
V  T  G  L  T  S (A) T  H  T  V  O  L
E  I  S  E  C  I  S  E  U  L  A  O  N
P  R  I  N  I  P  L  E  S  S  O
```

_ _____ ____

_____ ___

_____ _____

___ _____ ____

_____ ____ .

Dwight D. Eisenhower

57

42

```
  (L) T  U  S  E  E  C  T  N
 O  E  E  B  D  A  C  S  S  O  D
 O  F  H  E  H  N  U  E  O  T  L
 L  S  B  T  T  F  K  R  U  F  U
 F  T  U  R  O  L  U  F  E  S  O
    O  R  T  H  E  M  T  H  C
```

_ _ _   _ _   _ _   _ _ _ _ _ _ _

_ _ _   _ _ _   _ _ _ _ —.   _ _ _

_ _ _   _ _ _ _   _ _ _   _ _ _ _

_ _   _ _   _ _ _ _ _   _ _ _

_ _ _ _ _ _ —.

Mark Twain

58

```
      A  T  H  E  H  E  L  O  U
   H  U  T  H  W  L  Y  G  L  Y  R
   W  D  O  E  E  F  U  O  N  D  E
   W  O  Y  N  U  E  E (P) I  H  O
   O  T  N  R  I  S  S  R  E  T  I
      N  K  E  S  S  O  M  G  N
```

_ _ _ _ _ _ _   _ _
_ _ _ _ _ _ _   _ _ _   _ _ _ _
_ _ _   _ _ _   _ _ _ _   _ _ _ _
_ _ _ _   _ _ _   _ _ _ _   _ _ _ _ _
_ _ _ _ _.

Peyton Manning

59

```
    S  T  H  O  U  G  H  T  F
 A  R  W  O  N  N  E  W  S  O  S
(T) H  O  G  G  I  T  H  E  M  O
 H  G  N  A  S  H  H  S  L  N  E
 N  E  M  N  W  A  O  M  I  E  O
    O  T  I  E  M  L  B  O  T
```

— — —   — — —   — — —   — — — — —
— — — —   — — — — — —   — —
— — — — —   — — —   — — — — — —
— —   — — — — — —   — —   — — — — —
— —   — —.

Robert Bloch

60

```
    D  I  D  O  N  T  D  E  S  E  T  H
 N  S  I  T  I  H  T  E  R  E  E  V  A
 A  E  A  H  I  S  A  R  V  O  H  R  T
 V  R  T  R  A  W  R  E  N  T  D  T  E
 A  H  I  T  U  B  D  S  E  D (I) I
```

_   _ _ _ _'   _ _ _ _ _ _ _   _ _ _ _

_ _ _ _ _,   _ _ _   _   _ _ _ _

_ _ _ _ _ _ _   _ _ _   _

_ _ _ _'   _ _ _ _ _ _ _   _ _ _ _

_ _ _ _ _ _.

Jack Benny

61

```
L  A  C  I  N  H  C  E  T  O  R  A  E
I  E  F  I  S  O  R  A  N  E  F  R  E
T  N  I  L  T  F  L  A  A  T  T  L  H
Y  D  E  G  E  R  L  H  D  E  B  O  E
Ⓘ  O  B  I  O  N  S  I  T  O  W  T  H
```

— — — — — — — — — — — — — —
— — — — — — — — — —, — —
— — — — — — — — — — — —
— — — — — — — — — — — —
— — — — — — — — — — — —,

Bob Hope

62

```
K  E  R  F (F) R  E  O  W  O  H  H  A
A  S  E  E  E  D  M  O  T  R  T  V
T  K  D  H  T  E  I  N  S  E  O  D  I
S  E  A  O  M  U  D  S  T  N  T  N  G
I  M  M  O  T  L  C  N  I  O  I  F  I
```

_ _ _ _ _ _   _ _   _ _ _
_ _ _ _   _ _ _ _ _   _ _   _ _
_ _ _ _   _ _ _   _ _ _ _ _ _
_ _ _   _ _ _ _ _ _   _ _   _ _ _ _
_ _ _ _ _ _ _.

Mahatma Gandhi

63

```
Ⓦ  O  G  Y  E  H  T  A  A  L  C  U
L  A  E  B  C  A  O  M  S  P  D  A  R  C
L  T  C  Y  E  S  U  S  E  B  N  B  T  E
B  N  A  R  S  B  E  H  Y  D  O  I  N  H
   E  H  E  O  E  A  S  T  O  S  T  O
```

_ _   _ _ _ _'_   _ _ _   _ _

_ _ _ _ _   _ _ _ _ _ _

_ _ _ _ _ _ _   _ _ _   _ _   _ _ _

_ _   _ _ _   _ _ _ _   _ _ _

_ _ _ _   _ _   _ _ _ _   _ _   _ _.

Will Rogers

64

```
D N Ⓘ H A V E I G O T P
E W A F E N A H T A E D C R
S I A S C A T H W B A T T A
T N H C O H C N T O E L I C
  E I N U L D E N N Y L A
```

— —   — — — —   — — —

— — — — — —   — — — — — —'

— — — —   — — — — —,   — — — —

— — — — —   — — — —   —   — — —?

— — — — — — — —   — — — —.

Mel Brooks

65

```
  D O D E N R A E L R B X
N A T F T S H O I O T U P I
E C N G O A T S W H W W T S
A W I T R A H H R E E R I H
  I T H E B T R O O M Ⓘ G
```

— ——— —— ——— ———
———————. ————'— ———
— —————— —— ————;
—————— ——— ———
———————.

Bob Hope

66

```
    N  T  A  G  Y  U  S  D  N  Y  M  T
  O  U  B  M  M  E  V (I) E  D  I  M  S  S
  W  I  B  L  E  N  E  A  B  O  T  T  H  O
  U  J  R  E  K  T  H  A  E  T  S  A  O  L
     S  T  M  A  A  L  B  E  T  H  W  I
```

_ ____ __ __ _

____ _____. ___

__ _ ____ ___

_____ ____. ____,

___ __ ____ __ ____.

Steve Allen

67

Ⓞ C E I D A E H D E R S
Y N E E E N H O L L A D O U
M R V I F I T D F A M L Y E
A N T I L S E E V O L N I G
I S E N T L W I T H A G O R

— — — —   — —   — — —   — — — —,
— — — —   — — —   — —
— — — — — —   — —   — — — —
— — — —   — —   — — — —   — — — —
—   — — — — — — —   — — — — — — —.

Lucille Ball

68

```
(A) T N A P S I T E G C S
 E I L S A A R T T O A H A A
 G N O W Y D U O D E C N T H
 T E L F T W N L E B E T U H
 S H A H E O R F O R H E T R
```

— ——— ———— ———————
————— ——— ————
————— ——— ————
——— — —————— —— ———
——— ————— ——.

Sir Winston Churchill

69

```
Ⓘ N P O U W N Y T H D A
O M A N O Y I A T N I I A S
A W I L I F S Y A N G S A K
K A E T N C T N N A W Y M A
S N O D G I H A T U O F I N
```

— — — — — — — — —, — — — — —
— — — — — — — — — — — — — — —,
— — — — — — — —; — — — — —
— — — — — — — — — — — — — — —,
— — — — — — — — — —.

Margaret Thatcher

70

```
T N E T L G A M U F I D
L A T I H A I R O F L S Ⓣ L
Y P G I U R C G O L A H W R
W S I N G O W O T W H R E O
A I T N F O R I T S S P E R
```

___ _____ __ ____

__ _____ _____

_____ _____

___ ___ ____ __

____ _____.

Bertrand Russell

71

```
T  O  I  T  N  O  T  R  I  P  N  A  M  U
O  N  A  T  E  C  N  I  W  O  S  L  H  H
T  R  R  T  O (T) F     R  S  U  D  T  E
E  R  R  U  O  E  N  I  T  E  B  O  I  T
E  S  T  I  A  L  M  A  T  E  T  L  M  I
```

— —   — — — — — —   — — —

— — — — — — — —   — —

— — — — — — — — —   — — — — — —

— — — — —   — —   — —   — — — —

— — —   — — — — —   — — — — — —.

Stephen Hawking

72

```
H   O   N   E   P   E   R  (F)  Y   S   H   A   I   R
P   U   C   L   L   A   O   O   A   D   A   H   A   N
T   B   A   I   S   T   S   F   R   E   T   F   T   D
W   G   N   U   T   C   I   L   F   R   D   E   A   F
O   R   O   T   E   N   O   A   N   R   E   G   N   I
```

— — —   — — — —   — — — — —

— — — —   — — —   — —

— — — — — — — — — —

— — — — — — —   — —   — — — —,

— — —   — — — —   — — — —

— — — —   — — —.

Johnny Carson

73

58

```
(A) H  Y  L  L  E  R  D  H  T  F  I
 G  L  A  P  E  A  N  E  A  E  A  N
 O  L  P  V  M  O  O  C  T  H  Y  H
 O  N  E  A  O  M     N  I  H  I  T
 D  B  E  D  H  N  Y  R  E  G  N  R
 O  O  K  S  T  H  E  A  T  R  U  E
```

— — —   — — — —   — — — — —   — — — —

— — —   — — — — —   — —   — — — — —;

— — — —   — — —   — — — — —   — — —

— —   — — — —   — — —   — — — — —

— — — — — — — —.

Ernest Hemingway

74

```
    L  E  O  F  I  M  A  D  E
 T  T  O  T  S  T  E  R  L  U  K
 I  W  Y  R  A  I  H  N  I  F  N
 S  L  H  E  S  K  I  T  A  C  I
 S  O  N  A  W  D  N  U  N  D  Y
 A  R  E  I  T  A  S  R  E  D  H
    W  E  H (I) C  T  A  N  W
```

— ———' —————————
——— — ——————
——————— ———————.
——— — ——— — ———
———— ——— —— —————
—— ——.

George Burns

75

```
    W  Y  E  H  O  S  S  I  Z  A
 U  O  I  H  S  T  E  E  T  E  L
 L  N  N  I  P  C  K  S  A  M  H
 D  R  O  A  N  A  T  E  I  N (T)
 U  T  R  C  T  U  P  R  M  E  S
 R  E  B  P  O  P  E  M  E  V  E
 N  O  V  Y  T  H  S  E  L  V
```

_ _ _   _ _ _ _ _ _   _ _ _   _
_ _ _ _   _ _ _   _ _ _
_ _ _ _ _ _ _   _ _   _ _ _
_ _ _ _ _ _ _   _ _   _ _ _ _
_ _ _ _ _   _ _ _ _   _ _ _ _   _ _
_ _ _ _ _ _ _ _ _ _.

W. C. Fields

76

```
    T   O   E   R   O   S   H   T   N   O
 (M) D   C   R   G   M   M   A   V   E   M
    Y   O   E   A   E   E   G   E   H   M   X
    U   B   V   V   M   X   S   L   I   E   I
    T   O   L   I   N   O   I   D   L   B   S
    H   W   T   S   H   T   L   T   N   T   E
    E   N   I   C   O   U   P   A   Y   H
```

—— —————— ———— ——

——— ————— —— ———,

——— ———— — ——————

——— ——— ———— ——

———— —— ——— ——————

——— —.

Walter Matthau

77

```
    O   Y   R   R   M   E   O   O   L   Y
  R   U   Y   A   A   K   I   K   M   A   H
  B   S   A   A   M   N   O   L   U  (W)  A
  E   E   G   Y   N   A   Y   U   O   E   T
  S   A   U   T   F   W   R   Y   R   V   T
  S   E   D   A   L   O   E   E   I   E   H
  O   W   I   L   H   I   S   Y   S   G
```

— — — — — — — — — — — — —
— — — — — — — —, — — — — — —
— — — — — — — — — — — — —; — —
— — — — — — — — — — — — — — —,
— — — — — — — — —
— — — — — — —.

Phyllis Diller

78

```
    T  K  A  T  I  C  I  A  I  E
  H  A  E  B  E  T  E  N  N  L  V
  I  N  R  T  O  I  V  E  R  E  E
  S  U  E  P  D  O  L  E  C  B  S
  W  S  T  I  R  E  P  A  N  I  W
  O  I  U  S  S  Y  A  E (S) H  A
  D  R  Q  I  E  H  S  S  H  T
```

_ _ _ _ _   _   _ _ _ _ _ _ _ _ _

_ _ _ _ _   _ _ _ _ _ _   _ _ _ _

_ _   _ _ _ _,   _ _   _ _   _ _ _ _ _

_ _ _ _ _ _ _ _   _ _   _ _

_ _ _ _ _   _ _   _ _ _   _ _ _ _.

Charles de Gaulle

79

```
D  I  R  O  T  G  N  I  O  E  R  R
T  D  E  O  F  N  W  H (D) O  Y  T  A
H  E  G  O  R  E  W  A  S  T  U  U  Q
A  T  K  Y  E  G  H  T  A  T  H  I  A
H  S  A  S  H  T  N  E  H  D  K  N  T
E  J  U  T  W  H  I  P  P  E  O  U
```

__   ___   _____   ____

____   ____   _____

_____   _____

___   __   ____   __   ____

_____   ___   _

_____?

Steven Wright

80

```
    O U G B U T Y O U G O T
    O O T G N V I R O L L T A
  T Ⓨ A T O I M L A F A B H
    U O B B E A N A L Y E A V
    O Y E T I T O P A B A S E
    Y N I L T L F O T O L A
```

— — —   — — — — —   — — — — —   — — —

— —   — — — —   — — — — — — —

— — —   —   — — — — — —,   — — —

— — —   — — — — —   — — — —   —

— — —   — —   — — — — — —   — — —

— —   — — —,   — — —.

Roy Campanella

81

```
H  E  I  N  T  H  E  I  R  F  A  U  L
(T) B  N  H  K  S  T  P  O  P  E  O  T
O  A  I  T  Y  I  H  E  L  E  T  R  B
U  B  G  C  E  E     T  I  S  A  H  U
T  E  N  I  H  T  E  B  I  Y  W  T  O
I  N  G  A  C  E  L  R  T  H  E  N  Y
```

— — —   — — — —   — — — — —

— — — —   — — — —   —

— — — — — — — — —   — —   — — — —

— — —   — — —   — — — —

— — — — —,   — — — —   — — — — —

— — —   — — — — —   — — — — —.

Henry Kissinger

82

```
E   V   E   T   S  (F)  A   L   I   S   T   H   E
H   I   H   E   I   O   R   U   I   D   N   I   H
C   A   E   B   T   H   W   D   R   V   I   H   I
O   T   S   H   O   A   F   O   S   E   C   H   G
T   H   C   O   I   C   E   S   P   I   A   E   S
M   I   R   F   E   L   B   I   S   O   T   I   T
```

_ _ _   _ _ _ _   _ _   _ _ _

_ _ _ _   _ _ _ _ _ _,   _ _ _

_ _ _ _   _ _ _ _ _ _ _ _ _   _ _

_ _ _   _ _ _ _ _ _   _ _   _ _

_ _ _ _ _ _ _   _ _ _   _ _ _   _ _

_ _ _ _ _ _ _.

Aristotle

83

```
    T   N   E   R   E   L   W   A   M   E   H   T
A   R   I   D   E   A   R   A   H   Y   G   O   T   I
N   P   E   S   H   A   E   O   W   S   I   O   T   E
D   B   E  (T)  N   I   W   E   P   E   B   N   G   V
S   O   T   T   Y   S   D   L   O   E   P   O   T   I
    O   M   E   D   A   L   I   K   E   T   O   G
```

_ _ _ _ _   _ _ _   _ _ _ _ _

_ _ _ _   _ _   _ _   _ _ _ _ _

_ _   _ _ _ _   _ _   _ _

_ _ _ _ _ _ _,   _ _ _   _ _ _ _

_ _ _ _   _ _   _ _ _ _   _ _

_ _ _ _   _ _   _ _   _ _ _ _.

Bill Clinton

84

```
S   I   Y   T   T   E   R   U   S
G   G   I   H   A   H   N   B   E
T   N   O   L   T   T   W   A   C
O   I  (E)  A   T   I   H   T   U
D   E   I   E   H   W   A   I   O
A   T   R   E   L   E   R   S   Y
L   I   H   A   E   A   E   T   R
W   Y   T   E   O   D   L   H   O
O   U   H   R   Y   U   I   T   Y
```

_ _ _ _ _   _ _   _ _ _

_ _ _   _ _ _ _   _ _   _ _ _

_ _ _ _ _ _,   _ _   _ _ _   _ _ _

_ _   _ _ _   _ _ _ _   _ _ _

_ _ _ _ _ _   _ _   _ _ _ _   _ _

_ _ _   _ _ _ _   _ _ _.

Alex Haley

85

```
    L   P   E   H   T   D   N   A   Y   O   I   R
  I   T   O   O   P   L   E   A   R   L   S   U   C   E
  C   I   Y   T   E   P   N   E   T   A   K   R   O   S
  I   R   V   E   H   N   G   I   G   I   I   E   M   S
  A   E   A  (E)  K   I   G   S   N   A   N   H   E   N
  N   S   S   A   J   O   I   C   H   G   T   D   I   A
```

— — — — — — — —   — —
— — — — — —. — — — — —   — — —
— — — — —   — — — —
— — — — — — — —   — — — — — — — —
— — —   — — —   — — — — — — — — —
— —   —   — — — —.

Will Rogers

86

```
Ⓨ T  U  S  I  H  T  A  C  U  O  Y  F  I
O  O  K  O  O  W  L  B  N  N  E  A  N  E
L  G  U  N  U  W  O  A  T  O  C  L  D  E
D  I  N  T  R  O  Y     H  N  O  E  K  S
W  N  T  E  G  E  E  T  H  T  I  T  I  E
H  E  Y  O  U  G  T  E  C  A  K  E  S  L
```

_ _ _   _ _ _ _ _   _ _ _'_ _

_ _ _ _ _ _   _ _ _   _ _ _ _

_ _ _   _ _ _   _ _ _ _   _ _ _

_ _,_ _ _   _ __   _ _ _   _ _ _ _.

_ _ _,   _ _ _ _,   "_ _ _   _ _   _ _ _

_ _ _   _ _ _ _   _ _ _ _   _ _ _."

Jerry Seinfeld

87

```
      E  T  D  O  D  I  L  I  W  T
   C  A  N  A  M  W  S  W  L  E  I
   H  U  W  R  I  O  R  B  A  T  R
   S  O  E  G  L  E  U  E  E  E  R
   T  P  O  R  L  P  U  S  R  O  G
   H  R  W  W  I (I) O  E  P  U  E
   A  U  O  H  T  H  W  S  W  O  H
   T  T  H  E  L  E  S  E  R  T
```

— ———— ——— —————
——— ———— ———— ———
————, ——— ————— ——,
———— ——— ———— ——
——— ——— ————— ———
—————— —— ———— ——.

Thomas Jefferson

88

```
      E   E   D   R   E   R   A  (I)  C   N   A
  F   D   R   O   S   T   T   O   W   E   T   S   S
  E   R   I   I   A   T   N   E   N   T   A   H   I
  N   T   M   E   O   U   R   A   K   A   T   S   A
  T   C   Y   S   A   T   A   F   R   E   R   E   N
  O   H   T   N   A   T   S   G   B   S   E   V   E
      A   S   D   U   R   I   N   T   H   E   R
```

— ———— —— —

————————— ————

————— "————————— ——

——— ————•" —— —

—————— ——————

———— ————— ———

——————————•

Steven Wright

89

```
U  W  O  G  T  O  D  E  A  T  A
P  B  R  N  E  O  Y  M  A  H  N
C  N  E  V  S  E  H  C  N  T  Y
A  E  C  I  N  W  A  E  E  S  O
P  N  Y  O  C  R  P  B  C  N  N
R  S  A  O (D) E  R  T  O  A  G
E  I  D  N  M  N  E  S  P  U  R
D  E  N  T  A  T  E  D  I  W  O
```

— — — — — — —   — — — —
— — —   — — — — —   — — —
— — — —   — —   — —   — —
— — — — — — — —,   — — —
— — — — —   — — —   — — — — —
— — — —   — —   — — —   — —   — — — —
— — — — — — — —.

Johnny Carson

90

```
    B  O  O  K  D  N  I  S  O  M  B  O
 A  D  O  S  I  T  F (I) M  E  T  E  D
 A  N  E  I  V  E  E  I  Y  R  U  Y  N
 E  R  V  R  D  U  L  A  T  E  T  R  S
 R  O  R  E  Y  E  C  T  E  V  H  N  O
 D  O  H  T  E  O  I  N  G  G  E  S  E
 N  A  M  O  H  T  T  N  I  O  I  T
```

— ———— ——————————

———— ————————.

———— ———— ———————

———— —— ——— ———, —

—— ———— ——— ————

——— ——— ———— —

— — — —.

Groucho Marx

91

```
N  O  D  E  B  O  T  D  N  O  D  O  D
E  P  S  M  A  K  E  E  T  N  E  R  O
O  M  U  R  S  G  N  I  E  I  D  T  T
(C) T  E  U  B  H  I  T  A  S  O  O  R
F  T  M  T  T  O  T  O  E  A  A  S  E
T  O  S  O  F  N  G  E  L  M  A  E  I
H  E  T  H  I  S  T  H  Y  K  E  I  T
```

_ _ _ _ _ _ _   _ _ _ _   _ _

_ _ _ _ _   _ _   _ _   _   _ _ _

_ _   _ _ _ _ _ _,   _ _ _   _ _ _ _

_ _   _ _ _   _ _ _ _ _   _ _ _ _

_ _ _ _   _ _ _   _ _ _ _ _ _   _ _

_ _   _ _ _ _   _ _ _ _   _ _   _ _

_ _ _ _.

Andy Rooney

92

```
M  P  Y  I  T  N  K  I  N  K  O  F
E  F  T  H  I  O  H  G  I  B  H  T
L  H  E  M  O  F  T  E  L  O  O  E
A  S  P  E  S  H  T  P  E  P  T  G
A  P  O  L  U  E     O  E  M  S  L
S  A  L  L  H  F  G  L  O (S) A  A
S  G  L  E  T  I  F  A  S  S  S  S
E  H  T  F  O  K  N  L  A  H  S  A
```

____   _____   _____

__   ___   _____   __

____   ____.   ____

_____   _____   __   ___

_____   __   ____   _____

_   _____   __   ___

_____   __   ___   ___.

George Carlin

93

```
E  T  U  P  V  E (I) W  A  P  E
G  I  N  E  P  K  A  P  E  H  R
T  I  G  R  R  U  E  G  M  T  T
I  N  A  O  M  Y  N  O  R  N  H
N  T  T  G  R  I  N  R  O  I  E
O  N  O  N  D  A  B  F  A  O  L
S  Y  I  E  A  N  Y  R  U  A  O
I  N  M  N  E  P  B  I  T  T  K
E  M  A  F  I  G  A  O  E  H  T
```

— — — — — — — — — — — —

— — — — — — — — — — — — — — —

— — — — — — — — —

— — — — — — — — — — — — — —

— — — — — — — — — —

— — — — — — — — — — — — — — —

— — — — — — — — — — — — —, —

— — — — — —.

Benjamin Franklin

```
(I) H  E  R  T  O  K  M  E  T  O  H
 S  O  T  O  M  O  H  S  U  A  S  E  I
 T  E  P  P  X  W  E  W  L  D  E  N  M
 L  B  E  I  A  N  I  N  C  E  A  I  T
 I  E  D  S  S  A  T  A  K  A  P  N  S
 H  V  G  I  S  U  A  E  S  R  E  O  T
 P  I  N  N  T  Y  D  E  A  N  T  M  R
 A  R  G  O  M  R  O  F  H  D  A  E
```

_ _____ _____

__ ____ _____ ___

_ ___ ___. _____

___ __ __ ___ ___

__ _ _____

____ ___ __ ____

___ __ _____.

Shirley Temple

95

```
A  S  E  E  S  E  H  T  F  H  O  L
N  V  L  F  A  M  A  O  W  O  R  E
D  W  D  A  S  N  T  N  E  L  B  P
I  S  A  N  R  C  I  I  A  H  E  M
S  E  L  A  E  O     R  T (T) T  W
P  R  O  L  S  C  E  S  I  H  H  I
E  O  W  A  Y  S  T  D  L  E  T  S
P  O  F  T  A  H  O  F  R  O  W  T
L  E  S  O  F  U  L  L  D  O  U  B
```

_ _ _   _ _ _ _ _   _ _ _ _ _ _

_ _ _ _   _ _ _   _ _ _ _ _   _ _

_ _ _ _   _ _ _ _ _   _ _ _

_ _ _ _ _ _ _   _ _ _   _ _ _ _ _ _

_ _   _ _ _ _ _ _   _ _

_ _ _ _ _ _ _ _ _ _,   _ _ _

_ _ _ _ _   _ _ _ _ _ _   _ _

_ _ _ _   _ _   _ _ _ _ _ _.

Bertrand Russell

96

```
      M  S  P  E  E  K
   I  T  T  E  H  A  T
   T  N  I  E  I  T  U
   E  U  S  M  S  P  O
   S  A  R  U  M  A  R
   L  D  N  O  C  O  G
   O  S  E  S  H (A)
```

_ _ _ _ _ _ _ _ _ _ _ _

_ _ _ _ _ _ _ _ _ _ _ _ _

_ _ _ _ _ _ _ _ _ _ _ _ _

_ _ _ _ _.

Milton Berle

97

```
C  L  U  S  L  A  C  Y  O  U
N  O  N  O  I  P  W  E  E  G
C  K  N  I  T     E  H  R  O
(T) E  I  I  S  H  D  E  E  T
H  G  N  H  T  F  O  R  I  T
```

___ _____ __

___ _____ _____ ___

___ _____ __

_____.

Arthur Bloch

98

```
N  T  Y  N  M  E  R  A  N  W
G  I  H  A  H  (A) I  W  I  C  S  I
O  P  D  I  T  T  U  P  U  P  L  L
V  R  E  E  O  D  O  T  K  T  I  C
I  D  S  N  T  B  L  C  R  A  F  F
```

_ _ _ _ _ _ _ _   _ _ _ _   _ _ _

_ _   _ _ _ _   _ _ _ _ _ _ _ ,

_ _ _ _ _ _ _ _   _ _   _ _ _ _ _ _

_ _ _ _   _ _ _ _ _ _ _.

Dan Rather

99

(M) F O L O E I R T S
Y A R I S K S R N D
F L M E R S I E I A
O U U C L A E S L E
R S C Y W O R K A T

— — — — — — — — — — —
— — — — — — — — — — —
— — — —, — — — — — — — —, — — —
— — — — — — — —.

Paul Getty

100

```
T  I  O  N  O  F  J  U  D  U  I  R
M  C  L  L  O  C  P  E  C  I  Q  E
M  O  E  E  S  E     R  S  E  C  D
N  O (C) S  I  T  H  H  E  A  Y  B
S  E  N  N  E  E  T  G  I  E  G  A
```

_ _ _ _ _   _ _ _ _ _   _ _   _ _ _
_ _ _ _ _ _ _ _ _   _ _
_ _ _ _ _ _ _ _ _   _ _ _ _ _ _ _
_ _   _ _ _   _ _ _ _ _ _ _.

Albert Einstein

101

```
 I  I  A  T  H  T  S  T  E  A  E
 O  T  S  N  R  E  L  I  F  C  T  E  P
 N  R  O  U  B  L  E  U  E  N  D  A  S
 H  T  T  I  F  E  P  S  O  M  A  T  I
 A  T  S (L) I  S  L  E  A  S  H
```

— — — — — — — — — — — — —.

— — — — — — — — — — — — — —.

— — — , — — — — — — — — — — — —

— — — — , — — — — — — — — — — —.

Isaac Asimov

102

E I R U E R E O I E W E

Ⓘ E V N R L S U I D F R R

B I A E O B C S E T E N E

E L K Y U O W S L H R Y T

M E H T D L U O H U N A

— —————— —— ————.

——— ,— ——. —— ————

————— ——— ————,

——— ————— ——— —————

————?

Leo Durocher

103

```
I  E  A  S  I  D  E  A  D  A
R  L  S  P  T  T  G  I  L  A  R
E  K  I  T  U  H  H  A  S  S  K
H  V  E  H  C (D) I  T  I  I  T
T  E  I  T  E  E  C  D  E  D  H
E  R  S  N  F  O  R  S  A  N  O
G  O  T  E  U  E  H  T  D  L
```

_ _ _ _   _ _ _ _   _ _   _ _ _ _
_ _ _   _ _ _ _ _.   _ _   _ _ _   _
_ _ _ _ _   _ _ _ _,   _   _ _ _ _
_ _ _ _,   _ _ _   _ _   _ _ _ _ _
_ _ _   _ _ _ _ _ _ _ _
_ _ _ _ _ _ _ _.

Oprah Winfrey

104

```
Ⓘ  E  H  E  V  I  G  T  S  J  D  N
T  S  N  R  A  N  I  G  N  G  U  A  E
I  T  T  E  H  I  A  M  O  I  T  K  I
N  E  F  D  A  O  U  G  A  N  I  O  L
G  G  R  O  E  S  A  O  W  D  F  O  T
M  A  R  I  E  D  M  A  N  I  D  N
```

_ _ _ _ _ _   _ _   _ _ _ _ _ _

_ _ _ _ _ _   _ _ _ _,   _ _

_ _ _ _   _ _   _ _ _ _   _

_ _ _ _ _   _   _ _ _ _   _ _ _ _

_ _ _   _ _ _ _   _ _ _ _   _ _ _   _

_ _ _ _ _.

Rod Stewart

105

```
D  A  Y  T  D  I  P  O  W (T) N  I
I  N  N  D  H  I  T  U  T  H  I  E  T
A  M  O  A  M  U  S  N  I  F  N  I  T
B  E  N  T  E  A  N  G  S  A  R  E  H
U  O  R  U  S  S  R  E  V  I  N  U  E
T  T  H  E  U  N  I  V  E  R  S  E
```

___ _____ ___

_____ ___

_____ ___ _____

_____; ___ __'

___ ____ _____ ___

_____.

Albert Einstein

106

```
    D  H  I  S  I  N  H  E  R  N  A
 E  T  E  L  O  H  T  V  A  H  C  N  A
 R  S  D  E  E  E  E  E  O  L  O  G  M
 E  E  S  R  G  T  A  E  T  S  T  I  O
 T  M  E  H  E  S  H  B  H  I  A  S  W
 N  O  R  H  T  R  C  S  E  B  D  N  Y
    I  E (A) N  A  T  H  U  S  A  N
```

— — — — — — — — — — — — — —

— — — — — — — — — — — — —

— — — — — — — — — — — — — — —;

— — — — — — — — — — — — — — —,

— — — — — — — — — — — — — — — —

— — — — — — — — —.

Agatha Christie

107

```
I   G   O   T   O   W  (E)  E   R   L   O   O
R   E   T   S   R   E   H   O   V   K   Y   D   K
E   P   P   H   E   I   T   F   R   D   P   N   T
H   L   O   E   C   M   S   O   A   U   T   A   H
T   T   E   N   A   E   I   T   Y   E   U   O   R
O   M   I   I   R   L   E   I   G   G   H   T   H
N   F   I   A   C   I   S   B   R   O   F   E
```

_ _ _ _ _ _ _ _ _ _ _ _ _

_ _ _ _ _ _ _ _ _ _ _ _ _

_ _ _ _ _ _ _ _ _ _ _ _ _ _

_ _ _ _ _ _ _ _ _ _ _ _ _ _

_ _ _ _ _ _ _ _. _ _ _ _

_ _ _ _ _ _ _ _, _ _ _ _ _

_ _ _ _.

Robert Orben

108

Ⓘ N A P B A R O N A T N A W
M R C E L T Y D A N G O O U
I T E A S A U B I T A H N Y
S H I R B E E E S E P T L O
N L T O E T E D E D I K Y D
O L A F D A U P N N U G S T
N S E N S E B O E O H W H A

_,_ _ _____ __ ___
___ _____ _____
_____ ____ ___
____ ____. ____,_
____ _____. ____ __
___ ___ _? __
_____ _____?

Jean Kerr

109

```
U  S  A  I  N  I  R  U  D  S  U
R  S  E  G  L  G  E  N  Y  O  O
E  Y  I  F  A  R  B  I  R  U  I
O  L  L  I  A  R  M  R  S  C  O
U  T  A  E  N  F  I  S  E  N  C
R  E  H  G  R  D  N  A  U  F  N
I  E  N  H  A  A  L  A  L  A  I
N  S  U  I  T  S  E  G  T  T  M
O  S  C  H  A  R  B (S) O  R  E
```

— — — —   — — — —   — —   — — — —

— — — — — —   — —   — — — — — —

— — — — — — —   — — — — —

— — — — — —.   — —   — — — —

— — — —,   —   — — — — — — —   — — —,

— — — —   — —   — —   — — —

— — — —   — —   — — — — — —.

Fran Lebowitz

110

```
Ⓐ K  E  W  H  E  N  T  R  Y
N  G  C  A  E  L  P  O  E  T  A  I
I  E  E  O  M  M  I  S  A  P  H  N
H  N  M  O  N  T  E  T  K  T  S  G
T  E  U  M  T  E  L  F  O  E  L  T
T  M  I  I  F  Y  P  O  H  O  O  D
A  S  T  O  Y  O  M  C  I  T  S  E
E  U  O  R  O  L  F  C  G  N  E  I
R  N  O  L  P  O  E  T  O  M  M  G
E  D  T  S  I  F  E  L  P  O  S  N
```

— ————— ——————

———— ————— ————

——— ————— ——

————— ————————

—————————

———————— —— ——

—————————————— ———

———————— ——

——————— ————.

Douglas Adams

111

(O) U S T N A U R L R
N R R E T T N I A E
E D G A F   D H M S
L R E O O S T E O U
I H C R U S I E C R

___ _____
_____ _____ _.
___ _____ __ ___
_____.

Walt Disney

112

```
L  P  T  I  U  Q  E  W  E  B  G  N
A  R  O  W  O  B  C  A  S  E  N  Y  I
Y  G  W  L  D  E  S  U  C  O  O  A  L
I  E  D  O  W  E  W  U  A  D  Q  T  P
N  G  L  O  R  G  E (W) E  U  I  T
```

_ _   _ _   _ _ _   _ _ _ _

_ _ _ _ _ _   _ _ _ _ _ _   _ _

_ _ _ _   _ _ _,   _ _   _ _ _ _

_ _ _   _ _ _ _ _ _   _ _   _ _ _ _

_ _ _ _ _ _ _.

Oliver Wendell Holmes

113

```
S  H  C  H  A  S  B  U  O  T  H  I  G
I  F  G  N  E  I  T  N  S  I  E  N  C
L  O  I  N  C  N  R  N  O  R  B  N  A
O  N  A  K  I  G  A  D  E  T  E  A  C
I  D  O  T  I  D  T  B  E  H  E  R  C
K  A  F  N  A  E  O  N  I  L  W  E  O
T  N  H  M  Y  N  V  E  I  E  I  H  M
(W) A  C  C  N  O  W  L  T  V  T  W  P
L  H  E  A  U  L  D  T  U  H  E  D  L
L  A  T  A  G  N  I  K  A  O  H  S  I
```

— — — —   — — — —   — —   — — —
— — — —   — — — —   — — — —
— — — — —,   — —   — —   — — — — — —?
        ,
—   — — — —   — — — — — — — —   — —
— — — — —   — — — — — — —
— — — — — — —,   — — —   — — — — — —.
— — —   — —   — — — — — — — — — — —.
— — — — — —   — — — — — —   — — —
— — — — — —   — —   — — —.

Charles Lindbergh

114

```
U  S  P  I  S  T  R  E  U  S
N  N  W  S  G  S  G  A  T  Q  E  A
O  O  C  A  U  L  O  D (I) L  U  S
D  O  T  O  O  O  K  S  G  E  I  A
K  O  L  S  T  P  U  I  P  K  S  L
```

_ _ _ _ _   _ _ _ _· _ _ _ _

_ _ _ _   _ _   _ _   _ _· _ _ _ _

_ _ _ _   _ _ _ _   _ _   _ _·

_ _ _ _   _ _ _ _ _   _ _   _ _

_ _ _ _ _ _·

Sir Winston Churchill

115

100

```
W  N  F  E  E  L  I  N  P (I) D  Y
O  O  I  T  A  O  S  G  A  B  O  S
Y  N  N  T  T  V  N  Y  T  A  Y  P
M  W  H  E  E  M  E  R  O  N  R  A
W  L  A  T  P  I  S  I  L  B  S  I
O  L  O  F  Y  L  E  M  A  R  O  E
```

— — — —   — —   — — — — — — — — —.

— — — — — — —   — —

— — — — — — — —   — — — — —   — -

— — — —. —   — — — — —

— — — — — —   — —   — — —

— — — — — — — —.

Wolfgang Amadeus Mozart

116

```
A  A  N  P  U  E  V  A  G  Y  H  T  N  E
L  E (M) Y  F  I  F  S  A  E  L  R  W  H
I  T  R  O  I  L  E  P  F  I  E  U  E  S
Z  O  N  D  O  D  L     O  E  P  R  S  S
E  O  W  H  W  E  T  H  R  E  O  A  U  E
H  C  L  O  S  E  E  Y  W  E  T  S  C  C
```

_ _ _ _   _ _   _ _ _ _'_

_ _ _ _ _ _ _   _ _ _   _ _ _ _ _ _

_ _ _   _ _ _   _ _ _   _ _ _ _ _ _

_ _ _   _ _ _ _ _   _ _ _ _   _ _ _ _

_ _   _ _ _ _ _ _ _   _ _ _ _

_ _ _ _   _ _ _ _   _ _.

Thomas A. Edison

117

```
N  E  A (M) A  T  I  L  A  I
T  N  V  N  S  E  D  S  P  N
D  E  I  O  E     S  H  F  M
A  L  U  T  E  P  I  T  Y  O
N  G  A  G  N  E  E  D  O  C
```

— — —   — — — — — — —
— — — — — — —   — —   — — — — — —
— — —   — — — —   — — — —   — —
— — — — — — —.

Lily Tomlin

118

```
(I) D  E  D  Y  P  V  E  R  E  W
 N  M  N  O  B  O  E  I  W  S  H
 W  A  U  T  W  P  L  N  T  O  E
 T  O  S  A  R  E  U  H  N  K  N
 A  A  Y  Y  U  H  W  E  T  O  I
 N  R  D  N  O  W  O  T  N  S  T
 I  D  O  I  F  A  N  O  E  H  A
 H  C  N  U  O  T  H  G  U  D  R
```

__ , _____ __

_____ ___ ____ __

" ____ " ___ _____

____ ___ , ____

_____ __ ____ ____

___ _____

_____ .

Woody Allen

119

104

Below is an example of a Trickledown. The rules are simple; merely change one letter on each line to make a new word and continue until you reach the final word. We have provided two practice areas for each puzzle so you can write your possible solutions right in the book, if you choose.

Example:

MADE	**Answer:**	MADE
_____		MODE
_____		MORE
_____		WORE
WORM		WORM

Four-Letter Words:

PRACTICE:

1

PILL	PILL
_____	_____
_____	_____
_____	_____
DOOR	DOOR

PRACTICE:

2

SNOW	SNOW
_____	_____
_____	_____
_____	_____
PLAY	PLAY

3 **PRACTICE:**

MOST   MOST

_____   _____
_____   _____
_____   _____

HITS   HITS

4 **PRACTICE:**

BAND   BAND

_____   _____
_____   _____
_____   _____

PIPS   PIPS

5 **PRACTICE:**

PULL   PULL

_____   _____
_____   _____
_____   _____

BITE   BITE

6 **PRACTICE:**

DARE   DARE

_____   _____

_____   _____

_____   _____

BOLD   BOLD

7 **PRACTICE:**

HYPE   HYPE

_____   _____

_____   _____

_____   _____

CONS   CONS

8 **PRACTICE:**

POST   POST

_____   _____

_____   _____

_____   _____

MARK   MARK

9 **PRACTICE:**

CASH   CASH

_____   _____
_____   _____
_____   _____

LOOT   LOOT

10 **PRACTICE:**

MICE   MICE

_____   _____
_____   _____
_____   _____

LAMB   LAMB

11 **PRACTICE:**

COIN   COIN

_____   _____
_____   _____
_____   _____

SHOP   SHOP

12 **PRACTICE:**

DUDE   DUDE

_____   _____
_____   _____
_____   _____

MINT   MINT

13 **PRACTICE:**

MALT   MALT

_____   _____
_____   _____
_____   _____

BEER   BEER

14 **PRACTICE:**

PART   PART

_____   _____
_____   _____
_____   _____

TIPS   TIPS

15 **PRACTICE:**

LOST   LOST

_____   _____
_____   _____
_____   _____

MAPS   MAPS

16 **PRACTICE:**

PINK   PINK

_____   _____
_____   _____
_____   _____

SALE   SALE

17 **PRACTICE:**

PEST   PEST

_____   _____
_____   _____
_____   _____

BATS   BATS

18 **PRACTICE:**

PAST   PAST

_____   _____
_____   _____
_____   _____

FOUR   FOUR

19 **PRACTICE:**

BACK   BACK

_____   _____
_____   _____
_____   _____

RIDE   RIDE

20 **PRACTICE:**

WAND   WAND

_____   _____
_____   _____
_____   _____

RUST   RUST

21

PRACTICE:

CARE   CARE

——————   ——————

——————   ——————

——————   ——————

DIET   DIET

22

PRACTICE:

TAKE   TAKE

——————   ——————

——————   ——————

——————   ——————

RIPS   RIPS

23

PRACTICE:

MARE   MARE

——————   ——————

——————   ——————

——————   ——————

NODS   NODS

24

PRACTICE:

MOOD   MOOD

—————   —————
—————   —————
—————   —————

TURN   TURN

25

PRACTICE:

TORT   TORT

—————   —————
—————   —————
—————   —————

BAGS   BAGS

26

PRACTICE:

MEAN   MEAN

—————   —————
—————   —————
—————   —————

WORM   WORM

27

PRACTICE:

MOVE

_____

_____

_____

CARS

MOVE

_____

_____

_____

CARS

28

PRACTICE:

POPS

_____

_____

_____

CUTE

POPS

_____

_____

_____

CUTE

29

PRACTICE:

BELT

_____

_____

_____

DUEL

BELT

_____

_____

_____

DUEL

30

PRACTICE:

BALD   BALD

_____   _____
_____   _____
_____   _____

TIRE   TIRE

31

PRACTICE:

BAND   BAND

_____   _____
_____   _____
_____   _____

LORE   LORE

32

PRACTICE:

PARK   PARK

_____   _____
_____   _____
_____   _____

REST   REST

33 **PRACTICE:**

HARD   HARD

_____   _____

_____   _____

_____   _____

DIVE   DIVE

34 **PRACTICE:**

FEAR   FEAR

_____   _____

_____   _____

_____   _____

BOND   BOND

35 **PRACTICE:**

TOOK   TOOK

_____   _____

_____   _____

_____   _____

RACE   RACE

36 **PRACTICE:**

LAME   LAME

——————   ——————
——————   ——————
——————   ——————

PINT   PINT

37 **PRACTICE:**

HATE   HATE

——————   ——————
——————   ——————
——————   ——————

KISS   KISS

38 **PRACTICE:**

ZANY   ZANY

——————   ——————
——————   ——————
——————   ——————

MICE   MICE

39 **PRACTICE:**

FAST   FAST

_____   _____

_____   _____

_____   _____

MIND   MIND

40 **PRACTICE:**

FLAW   FLAW

_____   _____

_____   _____

_____   _____

SPOT   SPOT

41 **PRACTICE:**

SWIM   SWIM

_____   _____

_____   _____

_____   _____

PLUG   PLUG

42

PRACTICE:

CATS   CATS

_____   _____

_____   _____

_____   _____

NONE   NONE

43

PRACTICE:

BALL   BALL

_____   _____

_____   _____

_____   _____

FIRE   FIRE

44

PRACTICE:

MEAL   MEAL

_____   _____

_____   _____

_____   _____

HOST   HOST

45 **PRACTICE:**

FIST   FIST

_____   _____
_____   _____
_____   _____

GALL   GALL

46 **PRACTICE:**

GRAM   GRAM

_____   _____
_____   _____
_____   _____

CLOD   CLOD

47 **PRACTICE:**

TOWN   TOWN

_____   _____
_____   _____
_____   _____

BARE   BARE

48

PRACTICE:

MATH   MATH

_____   _____
_____   _____
_____   _____

BOYS   BOYS

49

PRACTICE:

PLUG   PLUG

_____   _____
_____   _____
_____   _____

STAY   STAY

50

PRACTICE:

VOTE   VOTE

_____   _____
_____   _____
_____   _____

TIPS   TIPS

51 **PRACTICE:**

LAME   LAME

_____   _____
_____   _____
_____   _____

SORT   SORT

52 **PRACTICE:**

LEGS   LEGS

_____   _____
_____   _____
_____   _____

PINE   PINE

53 **PRACTICE:**

MOTH   MOTH

_____   _____
_____   _____
_____   _____

BANE   BANE

54

PRACTICE:

VASE   VASE

_____   _____
_____   _____
_____   _____

CORD   CORD

55

PRACTICE:

MESS   MESS

_____   _____
_____   _____
_____   _____

LOOT   LOOT

56

PRACTICE:

FIND   FIND

_____   _____
_____   _____
_____   _____

MARE   MARE

57 **PRACTICE:**

PEAS   PEAS

_____   _____

_____   _____

_____   _____

SILL   SILL

58 **PRACTICE:**

CAST   CAST

_____   _____

_____   _____

_____   _____

BONE   BONE

59 **PRACTICE:**

CAMP   CAMP

_____   _____

_____   _____

_____   _____

SITE   SITE

60 **PRACTICE:**

FACT   FACT

_____   _____
_____   _____
_____   _____

PURE   PURE

61 **PRACTICE:**

FOLD   FOLD

_____   _____
_____   _____
_____   _____

BARE   BARE

62 **PRACTICE:**

TONE   TONE

_____   _____
_____   _____
_____   _____

LAUD   LAUD

63 **PRACTICE:**

BILL   BILL

_____   _____

_____   _____

_____   _____

MANE   MANE

64 **PRACTICE:**

GAME   GAME

_____   _____

_____   _____

_____   _____

SONG   SONG

65 **PRACTICE:**

HITS   HITS

_____   _____

_____   _____

_____   _____

BARD   BARD

66 **PRACTICE:**

LIST   LIST

_____   _____
_____   _____
_____   _____

MAPS   MAPS

67 **PRACTICE:**

TACT   TACT

_____   _____
_____   _____
_____   _____

POLE   POLE

68 **PRACTICE:**

DARE   DARE

_____   _____
_____   _____
_____   _____

TOUT   TOUT

69 **PRACTICE:**

WISP   WISP

—————   —————
—————   —————
—————   —————

ROPE   ROPE

70 **PRACTICE:**

SEED   SEED

—————   —————
—————   —————
—————   —————

ROAM   ROAM

71 **PRACTICE:**

FORM   FORM

—————   —————
—————   —————
—————   —————

WAND   WAND

72

PRACTICE:

WISH   WISH

_____   _____
_____   _____
_____   _____

HARP   HARP

73

PRACTICE:

BIND   BIND

_____   _____
_____   _____
_____   _____

DARN   DARN

74

PRACTICE:

LAME   LAME

_____   _____
_____   _____
_____   _____

SONG   SONG

75 **PRACTICE:**

ZOOM   ZOOM

_____   _____
_____   _____
_____   _____

MUMS   MUMS

76 **PRACTICE:**

HOOT   HOOT

_____   _____
_____   _____
_____   _____

CARP   CARP

77 **PRACTICE:**

MASK   MASK

_____   _____
_____   _____
_____   _____

COLT   COLT

78 **PRACTICE:**

PALL   PALL

_____   _____
_____   _____
_____   _____

CUTS   CUTS

79 **PRACTICE:**

FOOD   FOOD

_____   _____
_____   _____
_____   _____

SAIL   SAIL

80 **PRACTICE:**

JACK   JACK

_____   _____
_____   _____
_____   _____

ROOM   ROOM

81 **PRACTICE:**

TYPE   TYPE

_____   _____
_____   _____
_____   _____

CARS   CARS

82 **PRACTICE:**

MILK   MILK

_____   _____
_____   _____
_____   _____

FOND   FOND

83 **PRACTICE:**

DIME   DIME

_____   _____
_____   _____
_____   _____

TOLL   TOLL

84 **PRACTICE:**

PINT   PINT

_____   _____
_____   _____
_____   _____

GUTS   GUTS

85 **PRACTICE:**

WARS   WARS

_____   _____
_____   _____
_____   _____

MOLT   MOLT

86 **PRACTICE:**

YULE   YULE

_____   _____
_____   _____
_____   _____

MART   MART

87 **PRACTICE:**

DIME   DIME

———————   ———————
———————   ———————
———————   ———————

ROTS   ROTS

88 **PRACTICE:**

DIME   DIME

———————   ———————
———————   ———————
———————   ———————

RAYS   RAYS

89 **PRACTICE:**

PALM   PALM

———————   ———————
———————   ———————
———————   ———————

FOIL   FOIL

90 **PRACTICE:**

MIST   MIST

_____   _____
_____   _____
_____   _____

COAL   COAL

91 **PRACTICE:**

NEST   NEST

_____   _____
_____   _____
_____   _____

PACE   PACE

92 **PRACTICE:**

MAKE   MAKE

_____   _____
_____   _____
_____   _____

WORD   WORD

93 **PRACTICE:**

DIME   DIME

_____   _____
_____   _____
_____   _____

MALT   MALT

94 **PRACTICE:**

PALM   PALM

_____   _____
_____   _____
_____   _____

BITE   BITE

95 **PRACTICE:**

WANT   WANT

_____   _____
_____   _____
_____   _____

FORM   FORM

96

PRACTICE:

NEST   NEST

_____   _____
_____   _____
_____   _____

BUNS   BUNS

97

PRACTICE:

BOOM   BOOM

_____   _____
_____   _____
_____   _____

READ   READ

98

PRACTICE:

TARP   TARP

_____   _____
_____   _____
_____   _____

BONE   BONE

99 **PRACTICE:**

RACE   RACE

_____   _____

_____   _____

_____   _____

FIST   FIST

100 **PRACTICE:**

BOOM   BOOM

_____   _____

_____   _____

_____   _____

TURN   TURN

101 **PRACTICE:**

LAWN   LAWN

_____   _____

_____   _____

_____   _____

DIRE   DIRE

102

PRACTICE:

HEEL   HEEL

_____   _____
_____   _____
_____   _____

SHOD   SHOD

103

PRACTICE:

CROW   CROW

_____   _____
_____   _____
_____   _____

BLED   BLED

104

PRACTICE:

COAT   COAT

_____   _____
_____   _____
_____   _____

VASE   VASE

106 **PRACTICE:**

BEST   BEST

_____   _____

_____   _____

_____   _____

WILL   WILL

107 **PRACTICE:**

FOUL   FOUL

_____   _____

_____   _____

_____   _____

CLOT   CLOT

108 **PRACTICE:**

HUNT   HUNT

_____   _____

_____   _____

_____   _____

BASH   BASH

109 **PRACTICE:**

JUMP   JUMP

_____   _____

_____   _____

_____   _____

DARE   DARE

110 **PRACTICE:**

CLOD   CLOD

_____   _____

_____   _____

_____   _____

SKIT   SKIT

111 **PRACTICE:**

BOAT   BOAT

_____   _____

_____   _____

_____   _____

DIBS   DIBS

112

PRACTICE:

FOAL

_____

_____

_____

HAIR

FOAL

_____

_____

_____

HAIR

113

PRACTICE:

CLIP

_____

_____

_____

SHOD

CLIP

_____

_____

_____

SHOD

114

PRACTICE:

POOL

_____

_____

_____

CHAT

POOL

_____

_____

_____

CHAT

115

PRACTICE:

FOOT   FOOT

_____   _____

_____   _____

_____   _____

TARP   TARP

116

PRACTICE:

PEEL   PEEL

_____   _____

_____   _____

_____   _____

ROAD   ROAD

117

PRACTICE:

RACE   RACE

_____   _____

_____   _____

_____   _____

PINT   PINT

118 **PRACTICE:**

TOOL   TOOL

———————   ———————
———————   ———————
———————   ———————

RULE   RULE

119 **PRACTICE:**

PUPS   PUPS

———————   ———————
———————   ———————
———————   ———————

CONE   CONE

120 **PRACTICE:**

BURP   BURP

———————   ———————
———————   ———————
———————   ———————

GEMS   GEMS

121

PRACTICE:

SIFT   SIFT

_____   _____
_____   _____
_____   _____

RANK   RANK

122

PRACTICE:

PORT   PORT

_____   _____
_____   _____
_____   _____

CAPE   CAPE

123

PRACTICE:

PELT   PELT

_____   _____
_____   _____
_____   _____

MAIL   MAIL

Five-Letter Words:

124 **PRACTICE:**

CHOPS   CHOPS

_____   _____
_____   _____
_____   _____
_____   _____

SLATE   SLATE

125 **PRACTICE:**

SCARE   SCARE

_____   _____
_____   _____
_____   _____
_____   _____

CHILL   CHILL

126

PRACTICE:

FLEET   FLEET

_____   _____
_____   _____
_____   _____
_____   _____

STRIP   STRIP

127

PRACTICE:

CRUSH   CRUSH

_____   _____
_____   _____
_____   _____
_____   _____

SLAMS   SLAMS

128

PRACTICE:

GOODY   GOODY

_____   _____
_____   _____
_____   _____
_____   _____

MILES   MILES

129 **PRACTICE:**

CREST CREST

_____ _____

_____ _____

_____ _____

_____ _____

SHOWS SHOWS

130 **PRACTICE:**

BROWN BROWN

_____ _____

_____ _____

_____ _____

_____ _____

CHIPS CHIPS

131 **PRACTICE:**

MISTY MISTY

_____ _____

_____ _____

_____ _____

_____ _____

RUNGS RUNGS

132

PRACTICE:

TAPED	TAPED
_____	_____
_____	_____
_____	_____
_____	_____
CORNS	CORNS

133

PRACTICE:

BLOWN	BLOWN
_____	_____
_____	_____
_____	_____
_____	_____
STABS	STABS

134

PRACTICE:

THANK	THANK
_____	_____
_____	_____
_____	_____
_____	_____
SPIRE	SPIRE

135

PRACTICE:

SLANG   SLANG

_____   _____

_____   _____

_____   _____

_____   _____

TWICE   TWICE

136

PRACTICE:

GLOOM   GLOOM

_____   _____

_____   _____

_____   _____

_____   _____

BREAD   BREAD

137

PRACTICE:

STARE   STARE

_____   _____

_____   _____

_____   _____

_____   _____

PHONY   PHONY

138

PRACTICE:

CRASH   CRASH

_____   _____

_____   _____

_____   _____

_____   _____

SLUMS   SLUMS

139

PRACTICE:

GRASP   GRASP

_____   _____

_____   _____

_____   _____

_____   _____

CLIPS   CLIPS

140

PRACTICE:

THING   THING

_____   _____

_____   _____

_____   _____

_____   _____

CLUCK   CLUCK

141

PRACTICE:

CRUSH   CRUSH

_____   _____

_____   _____

_____   _____

_____   _____

SLAPS   SLAPS

142

PRACTICE:

CLOCK   CLOCK

_____   _____

_____   _____

_____   _____

_____   _____

SPIRE   SPIRE

143

PRACTICE:

CROWN   CROWN

_____   _____

_____   _____

_____   _____

_____   _____

SHIPS   SHIPS

144

PRACTICE:

CLICK	CLICK
_____	_____
_____	_____
_____	_____
_____	_____
SPARE	SPARE

145

PRACTICE:

TWICE	TWICE
_____	_____
_____	_____
_____	_____
_____	_____
SPANS	SPANS

146

PRACTICE:

CRAMP	CRAMP
_____	_____
_____	_____
_____	_____
_____	_____
SLICE	SLICE

146

PRACTICE:

PARTY   PARTY

_____   _____
_____   _____
_____   _____
_____   _____

TOOLS   TOOLS

147

PRACTICE:

PENCE   PENCE

_____   _____
_____   _____
_____   _____
_____   _____

SLANT   SLANT

148

PRACTICE:

TRAIN   TRAIN

_____   _____
_____   _____
_____   _____
_____   _____

BLOND   BLOND

149

PRACTICE:

PATHS   PATHS

_____   _____
_____   _____
_____   _____
_____   _____

MISER   MISER

150

PRACTICE:

SHORT   SHORT

_____   _____
_____   _____
_____   _____
_____   _____

PRUNE   PRUNE

151

PRACTICE:

SLOPE   SLOPE

_____   _____
_____   _____
_____   _____
_____   _____

WHIMS   WHIMS

152

PRACTICE:

WOODY WOODY

_____ _____
_____ _____
_____ _____
_____ _____

FARMS FARMS

153

PRACTICE:

TRACK TRACK

_____ _____
_____ _____
_____ _____
_____ _____

SWINE SWINE

154

PRACTICE:

TRACK TRACK

_____ _____
_____ _____
_____ _____
_____ _____

GLIDE GLIDE

155

PRACTICE:

TRUCK	TRUCK
_____	_____
_____	_____
_____	_____
_____	_____
GLADE	GLADE

156

PRACTICE:

TWICE	TWICE
_____	_____
_____	_____
_____	_____
_____	_____
STUNG	STUNG

157

PRACTICE:

BLOCK	BLOCK
_____	_____
_____	_____
_____	_____
_____	_____
START	START

158

PRACTICE:

CHORD   CHORD

_____   _____
_____   _____
_____   _____
_____   _____

STAGE   STAGE

159

PRACTICE:

SCENT   SCENT

_____   _____
_____   _____
_____   _____
_____   _____

PLATE   PLATE

160

PRACTICE:

STONE   STONE

_____   _____
_____   _____
_____   _____
_____   _____

CHIPS   CHIPS

161

PRACTICE:

COINS   COINS

_____   _____

_____   _____

_____   _____

_____   _____

DARED   DARED

162

PRACTICE:

MOODY   MOODY

_____   _____

_____   _____

_____   _____

_____   _____

RULES   RULES

163

PRACTICE:

TILED   TILED

_____   _____

_____   _____

_____   _____

_____   _____

SORTS   SORTS

164

PRACTICE:

SHOOT
_____
_____
_____
_____
CLICK

SHOOT
_____
_____
_____
_____
CLICK

165

PRACTICE:

CRACK
_____
_____
_____
_____
SLING

CRACK
_____
_____
_____
_____
SLING

166

PRACTICE:

FINED
_____
_____
_____
_____
DUCKS

FINED
_____
_____
_____
_____
DUCKS

167

PRACTICE:

DROWN   DROWN

_____   _____
_____   _____
_____   _____
_____   _____

BLABS   BLABS

168

PRACTICE:

ATONE   ATONE

_____   _____
_____   _____
_____   _____
_____   _____

SHIRT   SHIRT

169

PRACTICE:

THINK   THINK

_____   _____
_____   _____
_____   _____
_____   _____

START   START

170

PRACTICE:

SCALE   SCALE

_____   _____
_____   _____
_____   _____
_____   _____

CHORD   CHORD

171

PRACTICE:

PARTY   PARTY

_____   _____
_____   _____
_____   _____
_____   _____

DINES   DINES

172

PRACTICE:

SHAME   SHAME

_____   _____
_____   _____
_____   _____
_____   _____

ACORN   ACORN

173

PRACTICE:

PHONE	PHONE
_____	_____
_____	_____
_____	_____
_____	_____
SCARF	SCARF

174

PRACTICE:

CLASP	CLASP
_____	_____
_____	_____
_____	_____
_____	_____
GROWS	GROWS

175

PRACTICE:

BLOWS	BLOWS
_____	_____
_____	_____
_____	_____
_____	_____
GRASP	GRASP

176 **PRACTICE:**

MINOR   MINOR

_____   _____
_____   _____
_____   _____
_____   _____

DUDES   DUDES

177 **PRACTICE:**

BELLY   BELLY

_____   _____
_____   _____
_____   _____
_____   _____

TOOTS   TOOTS

178 **PRACTICE:**

FLUSH   FLUSH

_____   _____
_____   _____
_____   _____
_____   _____

BRATS   BRATS

179 **PRACTICE:**

GRAND   GRAND

_____   _____

_____   _____

_____   _____

_____   _____

BLEEP   BLEEP

180 **PRACTICE:**

CROWD   CROWD

_____   _____

_____   _____

_____   _____

_____   _____

GLASS   GLASS

181 **PRACTICE:**

CHILL   CHILL

_____   _____

_____   _____

_____   _____

_____   _____

STARE   STARE

182

PRACTICE:

STUNT   STUNT

_____   _____
_____   _____
_____   _____
_____   _____

PAIRS   PAIRS

183

PRACTICE:

CHIMP   CHIMP

_____   _____
_____   _____
_____   _____
_____   _____

SLAPS   SLAPS

184

PRACTICE:

STORM   STORM

_____   _____
_____   _____
_____   _____
_____   _____

CHASE   CHASE

Six-Letter Words:

185 **PRACTICE:**

PASTOR   PASTOR

_____   _____
_____   _____
_____   _____
_____   _____
_____   _____

HOOKED   HOOKED

186 **PRACTICE:**

GLAZED   GLAZED

_____   _____
_____   _____
_____   _____
_____   _____
_____   _____

TRUCKS   TRUCKS

187

PRACTICE:

PLANET   PLANET

_____

_____

_____

_____

_____

CROCKS   CROCKS

188

PRACTICE:

SLICES   SLICES

_____

_____

_____

_____

_____

CRANKY   CRANKY

189

PRACTICE:

TRADED   TRADED

_____

_____

_____

_____

_____

CLOCKS   CLOCKS

190

PRACTICE:

THINKS   THINKS

_____   _____

_____   _____

_____   _____

_____   _____

SPARED   SPARED

191

PRACTICE:

TRICKY   TRICKY

_____   _____

_____   _____

_____   _____

_____   _____

CLANGS   CLANGS

192

PRACTICE:

TAILOR   TAILOR

_____   _____

_____   _____

_____   _____

_____   _____

FOOTED   FOOTED

193

PRACTICE:

THANKS   THANKS

_____   _____
_____   _____
_____   _____
_____   _____
_____   _____

SPIRED   SPIRED

194

PRACTICE:

TOOTED   TOOTED

_____   _____
_____   _____
_____   _____
_____   _____
_____   _____

SAILOR   SAILOR

195 **PRACTICE:**

LASSOS   LASSOS

_____   _____
_____   _____
_____   _____
_____   _____
_____   _____

PURGED   PURGED

196 **PRACTICE:**

PASTOR   PASTOR

_____   _____
_____   _____
_____   _____
_____   _____
_____   _____

TOURED   TOURED

1

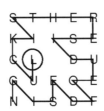

L U C K   I S   T H E   R E S I D U.
O F   D E S I G N.

Branch Rickey

2

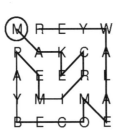

M A K E   C R I M E   P A Y,
B E C O M E   A   L A W Y E R.

Will Rogers

3

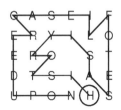

H I S T O R Y I S A S E T O F
L I E S A G R E E D U P O N.

Napoleon Bonaparte

4

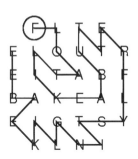

F L O A T L I K E A
B U T T E R F L Y, S T I N G
L I K E A B E E.

Muhammad Ali

5

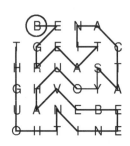

B E   G R E A T   I N   A C T,   A S
Y O U   H A V E   B E E N   I N
T H O U G H T.

William Shakespeare

6

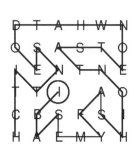

I   B A S E   M Y   F A S H I O N
T A S T E   O N   W H A T
D O E S N ' T   I T C H.

Gilda Radner

7

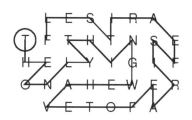

T H E   O N L Y   T H I N G   W E
H A V E   T O   F E A R   I S
F E A R   I T S E L F.

Franklin D. Roosevelt

8

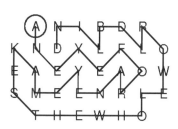

A N   E Y E   F O R   A N   E Y E
M A K E S   T H E   W H O L E
W O R L D   B L I N D.

Mahatma Gandhi

9

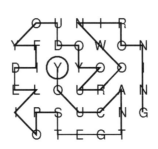

Y O U   C A N'T   G E T
S P O I L E D   I F   Y O U   D O
Y O U R   O W N   I R O N I N G.

Meryl Streep

10

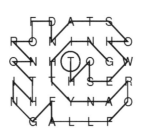

T H O S E   W H O   S T A N D   F O R
N O T H I N G   F A L L   F O R
A N Y T H I N G.

Alexander Hamilton

11

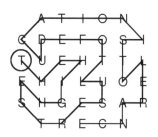

<u>T</u> <u>H</u> <u>E</u> <u>H</u> <u>I</u> <u>G</u> <u>H</u> <u>E</u> <u>S</u> <u>T</u> <u>R</u> <u>E</u> <u>S</u> <u>U</u> <u>L</u> <u>T</u>
<u>O</u> <u>F</u> <u>E</u> <u>D</u> <u>U</u> <u>C</u> <u>A</u> <u>T</u> <u>I</u> <u>O</u> <u>N</u> <u>I</u> <u>S</u>
<u>T</u> <u>O</u> <u>L</u> <u>E</u> <u>R</u> <u>A</u> <u>N</u> <u>C</u> <u>E</u>.

Helen Keller

12

<u>I</u>'<u>M</u> <u>S</u> <u>T</u> <u>R</u> <u>O</u> <u>N</u> <u>G</u> <u>T</u> <u>O</u> <u>T</u> <u>H</u> <u>E</u>
<u>F</u> <u>I</u> <u>N</u> <u>I</u> <u>S</u> <u>H</u>, '<u>C</u> <u>A</u> <u>U</u> <u>S</u> <u>E</u> <u>I</u> <u>E</u> <u>A</u> <u>T</u> <u>S</u>
<u>M</u> <u>E</u> <u>S</u> <u>P</u> <u>I</u> <u>N</u> <u>A</u> <u>C</u> <u>H</u>.

Popeye

13

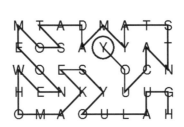

Y O U   C A N ' T   S T A Y   M A D
A T   S O M E O N E   W H O
M A K E S   Y O U   L A U G H.

Jay Leno

14

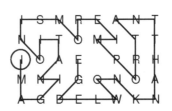

I M A G I N A T I O N   I S   M O R E
I M P O R T A N T   T H A N
K N O W L E D G E.

Albert Einstein

15

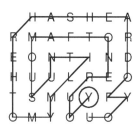

<u>Y</u> <u>O</u> <u>U</u>'<u>R</u> <u>E</u>   <u>N</u> <u>O</u> <u>T</u>   <u>F</u> <u>A</u> <u>M</u> <u>O</u> <u>U</u> <u>S</u>
<u>U</u> <u>N</u> <u>T</u> <u>I</u> <u>L</u>   <u>M</u> <u>Y</u>   <u>M</u> <u>O</u> <u>T</u> <u>H</u> <u>E</u> <u>R</u>   <u>H</u> <u>A</u> <u>S</u>
<u>H</u> <u>E</u> <u>A</u> <u>R</u> <u>D</u>   <u>O</u> <u>F</u>   <u>Y</u> <u>O</u> <u>U</u>.

Jay Leno

16

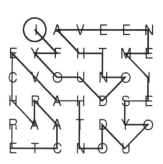

<u>I</u> <u>F</u>   <u>Y</u> <u>O</u> <u>U</u>   <u>D</u> <u>O</u> <u>N</u>'<u>T</u>   <u>H</u> <u>A</u> <u>V</u> <u>E</u>
<u>E</u> <u>N</u> <u>E</u> <u>M</u> <u>I</u> <u>E</u> <u>S</u>,   <u>Y</u> <u>O</u> <u>U</u>   <u>D</u> <u>O</u> <u>N</u>'<u>T</u>
<u>H</u> <u>A</u> <u>V</u> <u>E</u>   <u>C</u> <u>H</u> <u>A</u> <u>R</u> <u>A</u> <u>C</u> <u>T</u> <u>E</u> <u>R</u>.

Paul Newman

179

17

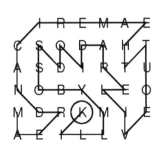

K I L L   M Y   B O S S?   D O   I
D A R E   L I V E   O U T   T H E
A M E R I C A N   D R E A M?

Homer Simpson

18

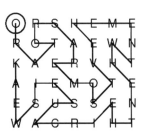

O R A T O R S   A R E   M O S T
V E H E M E N T   W H E N   T H E I R
C A U S E   I S   W E A K.

Cicero

19

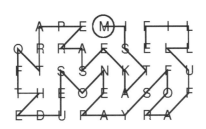

M I S T A K E S   A R E   P A R T
O F   T H E   D U E S   O N E
P A Y S   F O R   A   F U L L
L I F E.

Sophia Loren

20

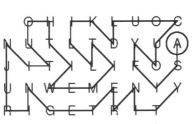

A S   I F   Y O U   C O U L D
K I L L   T I M E   W I T H O U T
I N J U R I N G   E T E R N I T Y.

Henry David Thoreau

21

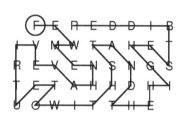

F E W   M E N   H A V E   V I R T U E
T O   W I T H S T A N D   T H E
H I G H E S T   B I D D E R.

George Washington

22

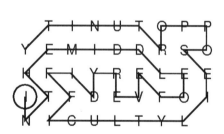

I N   T H E   M I D D L E   O F
E V E R Y   D I F F I C U L T Y
L I E S   O P P O R T U N I T Y.

Albert Einstein

23

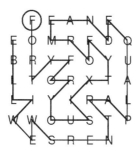

F O R T Y   F O R   Y O U,   S I X T Y
F O R   M E.   A N D   E Q U A L
P A R T N E R S   W E   W I L L   B E.

Joan Rivers

24

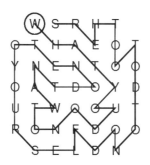

W H A T   Y O U   D O   N O T
W A N T   D O N E   T O
Y O U R S E L F,   D O   N O T   D O
T O   O T H E R S.

Confucius

25

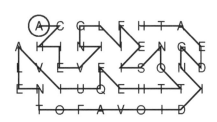

A C H I E V I N G   L I F E   I S
N O T   T H E   E Q U I V A L E N T
O F   A V O I D I N G   D E A T H.

Ayn Rand

26

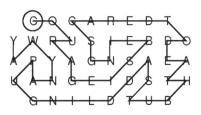

C O U R A G E   I S   B E I N G
S C A R E D   T O   D E A T H   B U T
S A D D L I N G   U P   A N Y W A Y.

John Wayne

27

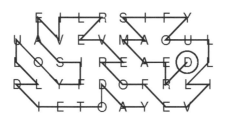

D R E A M   A S   I F   Y O U ' L L
L I V E   F O R E V E R,   L I V E
A S   I F   Y O U ' L L   D I E
T O D A Y.

James Dean

28

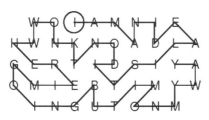

I   A M   A N   I D E A L I S T,   I
D O N ' T   K N O W   W H E R E   I ' M
G O I N G   B U T   I ' M   O N   M Y
W A Y.

Carl Sandburg

29

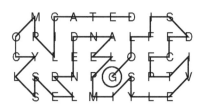

G O L F   I S   D E C E P T I V E L Y
S I M P L E   A N D
E N D L E S S L Y
C O M P L I C A T E D.

Arnold Palmer

30

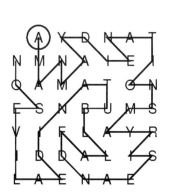

A   M A N   M A Y   D I E,
N A T I O N S   M A Y   R I S E
A N D   F A L L,   B U T   A N
I D E A   L I V E S   O N.

John F. Kennedy

31

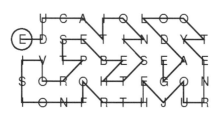

E D U C A T I O N   I S   T H E
B E S T   P R O V I S I O N   F O R
T H E   J O U R N E Y   T O   O L D
A G E.

Aristotle

32

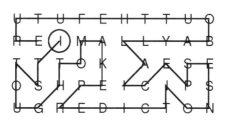

I T'S   T O U G H   T O   M A K E
P R E D I C T I O N S,
E S P E C I A L L Y   A B O U T
T H E   F U T U R E.

Yogi Berra

33

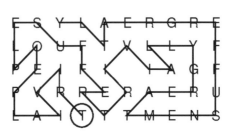

T R I V I A L   P E O P L E
S U F F E R   T R I V I A L L Y,
G R E A T   M E N   S U F F E R
G R E A T L Y.

Bertrand Russell

34

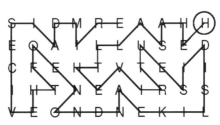

H E   H A S   A L L   T H E
V I R T U E S   I   D I S L I K E
A N D   N O N E   O F   T H E
V I C E S   I   A D M I R E.

Sir Winston Churchill

35

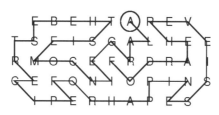

A LARGE INCOME IS
THE BEST RECIPE FOR
HAPPINESS I EVER
HEARD OF.

Jane Austen

36

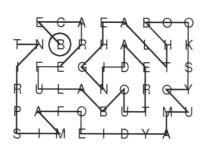

BE CAREFUL ABOUT
READING HEALTH
BOOKS. YOU MAY DIE
OF A MISPRINT.

Mark Twain

37

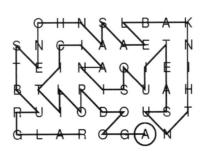

A GOOD POLITICIAN IS QUITE AS UNTHINKABLE AS AN HONEST BURGLAR.

H. L. Mencken

38

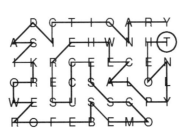

THE ONLY PLACE WHERE SUCCESS COMES BEFORE WORK IS A DICTIONARY.

Vidal Sassoon

39

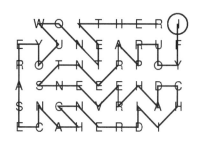

I F   Y O U R   P A R E N T S
N E V E R   H A D   C H I L D R E N,
C H A N C E S   A R E   Y O U
W O N'T   E I T H E R.

Dick Cavett

40

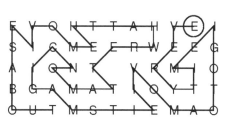

E V E R Y   T I M E   I   G O   T O
A   M O V I E,   I T'S   M A G I C,
N O   M A T T E R   W H A T   T H E
M O V I E'S   A B O U T.

Steven Spielberg

41

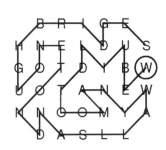

W E   B U I L D   T O O   M A N Y
W A L L S   A N D   N O T
E N O U G H   B R I D G E S.

Sir Isaac Newton

42

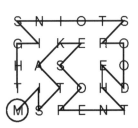

M I S T A K E S   O P E N   T H E
D O O R S   T O   I N S I G H T.

Terry Stickels

43

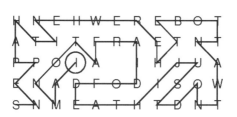

I AM NOT AFRAID OF
DEATH. I JUST DON'T
WANT TO BE THERE
WHEN IT HAPPENS.

Woody Allen

44

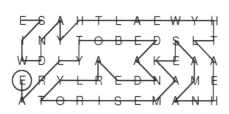

EARLY TO BED AND
EARLY TO RISE MAKES
A MAN HEALTHY,
WEALTHY, AND WISE.

Benjamin Franklin

45

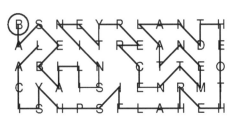

B A S E B A L L   I S   N I N E T Y
P E R C E N T   M E N T A L   A N D
T H E   O T H E R   H A L F   I S
P H Y S I C A L.

Yogi Berra

46

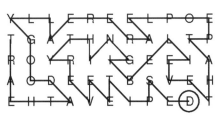

D E S P I T E   E V E R Y T H I N G,
I   B E L I E V E   T H A T
P E O P L E   A R E   R E A L L Y
G O O D   A T   H E A R T.

Anne Frank

47

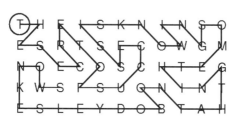

T H E   S E C R E T   O F
S U C C E S S   I S   K N O W I N G
S O M E T H I N G   T H A T
N O B O D Y   E L S E   K N O W S.

Aristotle Onassis

48

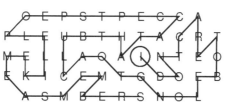

I   D O N'T   C A R E   T O
B E L O N G   T O   A   C L U B
T H A T   A C C E P T S   P E O P L E
L I K E   M E   A S   M E M B E R S.

Groucho Marx

49

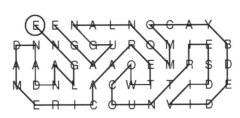

E N G L A N D   A N D   A M E R I C A
A R E   T W O   C O U N T R I E S
D I V I D E D   B Y   A   C O M M O N
L A N G U A G E.

George Bernard Shaw

50

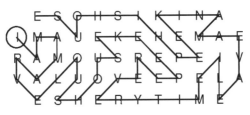

I   A M   A   M A R V E L O U S
H O U S E K E E P E R.   E V E R Y
T I M E   I   L E A V E   A   M A N
I   K E E P   H I S   H O U S E.

Zsa Zsa Gabor

51

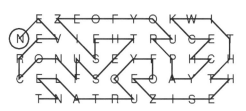

<u>N</u> <u>E</u> <u>V</u> <u>E</u> <u>R</u>   <u>C</u> <u>O</u> <u>N</u> <u>F</u> <u>U</u> <u>S</u> <u>E</u>   <u>T</u> <u>H</u> <u>E</u>
<u>S</u> <u>I</u> <u>Z</u> <u>E</u>   <u>O</u> <u>F</u>   <u>Y</u> <u>O</u> <u>U</u> <u>R</u>
<u>P</u> <u>A</u> <u>Y</u> <u>C</u> <u>H</u> <u>E</u> <u>C</u> <u>K</u>   <u>W</u> <u>I</u> <u>T</u> <u>H</u>   <u>T</u> <u>H</u> <u>E</u>
<u>S</u> <u>I</u> <u>Z</u> <u>E</u>   <u>O</u> <u>F</u>   <u>Y</u> <u>O</u> <u>U</u> <u>R</u>   <u>T</u> <u>A</u> <u>L</u> <u>E</u> <u>N</u> <u>T</u>.

Marlon Brando

52

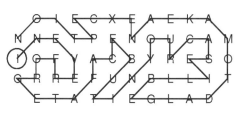

<u>I</u>   <u>N</u> <u>E</u> <u>V</u> <u>E</u> <u>R</u>   <u>F</u> <u>O</u> <u>R</u> <u>G</u> <u>E</u> <u>T</u>   <u>A</u>
<u>F</u> <u>A</u> <u>C</u> <u>E</u>,   <u>B</u> <u>U</u> <u>T</u>   <u>I</u> <u>N</u>   <u>Y</u> <u>O</u> <u>U</u> <u>R</u>
<u>C</u> <u>A</u> <u>S</u> <u>E</u>   <u>I</u>'<u>L</u> <u>L</u>   <u>B</u> <u>E</u>   <u>G</u> <u>L</u> <u>A</u> <u>D</u>   <u>T</u> <u>O</u>
<u>M</u> <u>A</u> <u>K</u> <u>E</u>   <u>A</u> <u>N</u>   <u>E</u> <u>X</u> <u>C</u> <u>E</u> <u>P</u> <u>T</u> <u>I</u> <u>O</u> <u>N</u>.

Groucho Marx

53

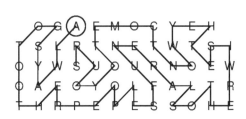

A L W A Y S   G O   T O   O T H E R
P E O P L E ' S   F U N E R A L S ,
O T H E R W I S E   T H E Y   W O N ' T
C O M E   T O   Y O U R S .

Yogi Berra

54

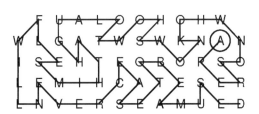

A   P E R S O N   W H O   K N O W S
H O W   T O   L A U G H   A T
H I M S E L F   W I L L   N E V E R
C E A S E   T O   B E   A M U S E D .

Shirley MacLaine

55

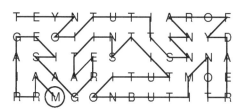

M A R R I A G E   I S   A   G R E A T

I N S T I T U T I O N,   B U T   I ' M

N O T   R E A D Y   F O R   A N

I N S T I T U T I O N   Y E T.

Mae West

56

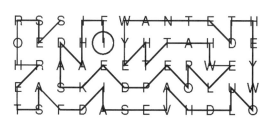

I F   I   H A D   A S K E D

P E O P L E   W H A T   T H E Y

W A N T E D,   T H E Y   W O U L D

H A V E   S A I D   F A S T E R

H O R S E S.

Henry Ford

57

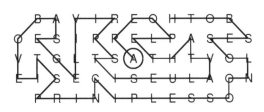

A PEOPLE THAT
VALUES ITS
PRIVILEGES ABOVE
ITS PRINCIPLES SOON
LOSES BOTH.

Dwight D. Eisenhower

58

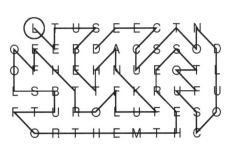

LET US BE THANKFUL
FOR THE FOOLS. BUT
FOR THEM THE REST
OF US COULD NOT
SUCCEED.

Mark Twain

59

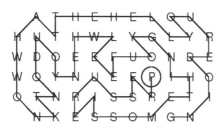

P R E S S U R E   I S
S O M E T H I N G   Y O U   F E E L
W H E N   Y O U   D O N ' T   K N O W
W H A T   T H E   H E L L   Y O U ' R E
D O I N G.

Peyton Manning

60

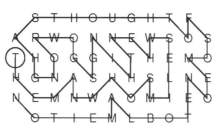

T H E   M A N   W H O   S M I L E S
W H E N   T H I N G S   G O
W R O N G   H A S   T H O U G H T
O F   S O M E O N E   T O   B L A M E
I T   O N.

Robert Bloch

61

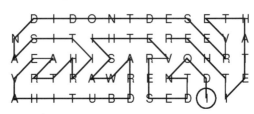

I DON'T DESERVE THIS
AWARD, BUT I HAVE
ARTHRITIS AND I
DON'T DESERVE THAT
EITHER.

Jack Benny

62

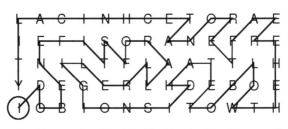

I DO BENEFITS FOR
ALL RELIGIONS. I'D
HATE TO BLOW THE
HEREAFTER ON A
TECHNICALITY.

Bob Hope

63

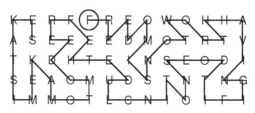

F R E E D O M   I S   N O T
W O R T H   H A V I N G   I F   I T
D O E S   N O T   I N C L U D E
T H E   F R E E D O M   T O   M A K E
M I S T A K E S.

Mahatma Gandhi

64

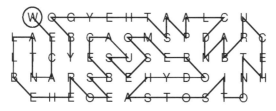

W E   C A N'T   A L L   B E
H E R O E S   B E C A U S E
S O M E B O D Y   H A S   T O   S I T
O N   T H E   C U R B   A N D
C L A P   A S   T H E Y   G O   B Y.

Will Rogers

65

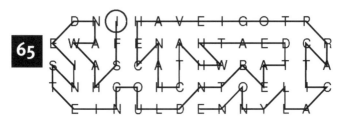

I F S H A W A N D
E I N S T E I N C O U L D N' T
B E A T D E A T H , W H A T
C H A N C E H A V E I G O T ?
P R A C T I C A L L Y N O N E .

Mel Brooks

66

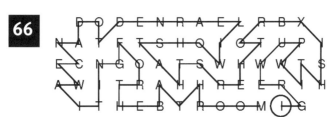

I G R E W U P W I T H S I X
B R O T H E R S . T H A T' S H O W
I L E A R N E D T O D A N C E ;
W A I T I N G F O R T H E
B A T H R O O M .

Bob Hope

67

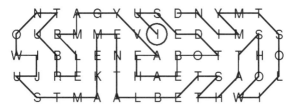

I USED TO BE A
HEAVY GAMBLER, BUT
NOW I JUST MAKE
MENTAL BETS. THAT'S
HOW I LOST MY MIND.

Steve Allen

68

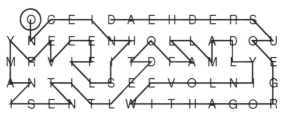

ONCE IN HIS LIFE,
EVERY MAN IS
ENTITLED TO FALL
MADLY IN LOVE WITH
A GORGEOUS REDHEAD.

Lucille Ball

69

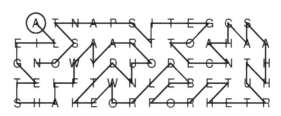

A LIE GETS HALFWAY
AROUND THE WORLD
BEFORE THE TRUTH
HAS A CHANCE TO GET
ITS PANTS ON.

Sir Winston Churchill

70

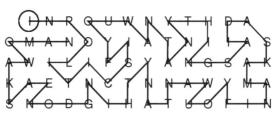

IN POLITICS, IF YOU
WANT ANYTHING SAID,
ASK A MAN; IF YOU
WANT ANYTHING DONE,
ASK A WOMAN.

Margaret Thatcher

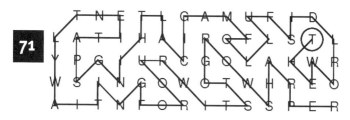

71

T H E   W O R L D   I S   F U L L
O F   M A G I C A L   T H I N G S
P A T I E N T L Y   W A I T I N G
F O R   O U R   W I T S   T O
G R O W   S H A R P E R.

Bertrand Russell

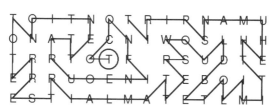

72

T O   C O N F I N E   O U R
A T T E N T I O N   T O
T E R R E S T R I A L   M A T T E R S
W O U L D   B E   T O   L I M I T
T H E   H U M A N   S P I R I T.

Stephen Hawking

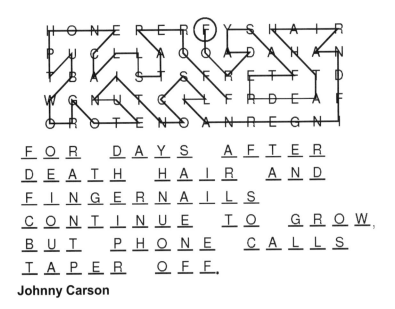

F O R   D A Y S   A F T E R
D E A T H   H A I R   A N D
F I N G E R N A I L S
C O N T I N U E   T O   G R O W,
B U T   P H O N E   C A L L S
T A P E R   O F F.

Johnny Carson

73

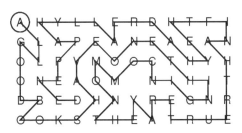

ALL GOOD BOOKS HAVE
ONE THING IN COMMON;
THEY ARE TRUER THAN
IF THEY HAD REALLY
HAPPENED.

Ernest Hemingway

74

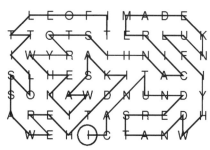

I CAN'T UNDERSTAND
WHY I FLUNKED
AMERICAN HISTORY.
WHEN I WAS A KID
THERE WAS SO LITTLE
OF IT.

George Burns

75

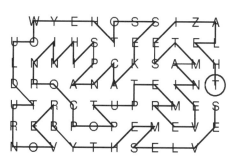

T H E   L A Z I E S T   M A N   I
E V E R   M E T   P U T
P O P C O R N   I N   H I S
P A N C A K E S   S O   T H E Y
W O U L D   T U R N   O V E R   B Y
T H E M S E L V E S.

W. C. Fields

76

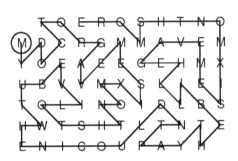

MY DOCTOR GAVE ME
SIX MONTHS TO LIVE,
BUT WHEN I COULDN'T
PAY THE BILL HE
GAVE ME SIX MONTHS
MORE.

Walter Matthau

77

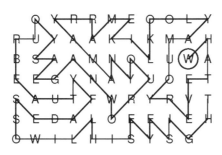

W H A T E V E R   Y O U   M A Y
L O O K   L I K E ,   M A R R Y   A
M A N   Y O U R   O W N   A G E ;   A S
Y O U R   B E A U T Y   F A D E S ,
S O   W I L L   H I S
E Y E S I G H T .

Phyllis Diller

78

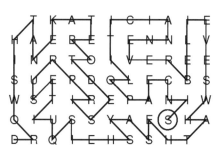

S I N C E   A   P O L I T I C I A N
N E V E R   B E L I E V E S   W H A T
H E   S A Y S,   H E   I S   Q U I T E
S U R P R I S E D   T O   B E
T A K E N   A T   H I S   W O R D.

Charles de Gaulle

79

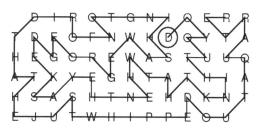

D O   Y O U   T H I N K   T H A T

W H E N   T H E Y   A S K E D

G E O R G E   W A S H I N G T O N

F O R   I D   T H A T   H E   J U S T

W H I P P E D   O U T   A

Q U A R T E R?

Steven Wright

80

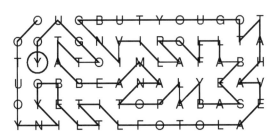

Y O U   G O T T A   B E   A   M A N
T O   P L A Y   B A S E B A L L
F O R   A   L I V I N G ,   B U T
Y O U   G O T T A   H A V E   A
L O T   O F   L I T T L E   B O Y
I N   Y O U ,   T O O .

Roy Campanella

81

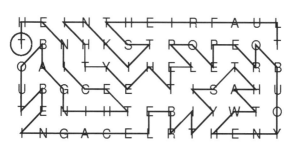

T H E   N I C E   T H I N G
A B O U T   B E I N G   A
C E L E B R I T Y   I S   T H A T
W H E N   Y O U   B O R E
P E O P L E,   T H E Y   T H I N K
I T ' S   T H E I R   F A U L T.

Henry Kissinger

82

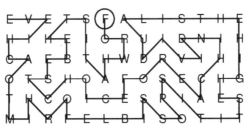

F O R   W H A T   I S   T H E
B E S T   C H O I C E,   F O R
E A C H   I N D I V I D U A L   I S
T H E   H I G H E S T   I T   I S
P O S S I B L E   F O R   H I M   T O
A C H I E V E.

Aristotle

83

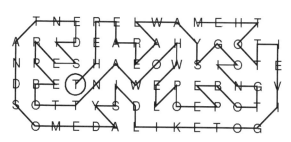

T H E R E   A R E   A L W A Y S
G O I N G   T O   B E   P E O P L E
W H O   W A N T   T O   B E
P R E S I D E N T,   A N D   S O M E
D A Y S   I'D   L I K E   T O
G I V E   I T   T O   T H E M.

Bill Clinton

84

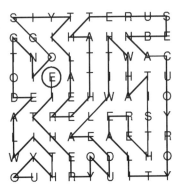

E I T H E R   Y O U   D E A L
W I T H   W H A T   I S   T H E
R E A L I T Y ,   O R   Y O U   C A N
B E   S U R E   T H A T   T H E
R E A L I T Y   I S   G O I N G   T O
D E A L   W I T H   Y O U .

Alex Haley

85

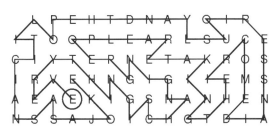

E V E R Y T H I N G   I S

C H A N G I N G.   P E O P L E   A R E

T A K I N G   T H E I R

C O M E D I A N S   S E R I O U S L Y

A N D   T H E   P O L I T I C I A N S

A S   A   J O K E.

Will Rogers

86

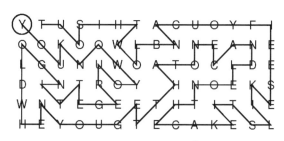

Y O U K N O W Y O U ' R E
G E T T I N G O L D W H E N
Y O U G E T T H A T O N E
C A N D L E O N T H E C A K E.
I T ' S L I K E, "S E E I F Y O U
C A N B L O W T H I S O U T."

Jerry Seinfeld

87

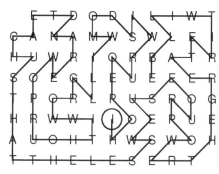

I HOPE OUR WISDOM
WILL GROW WITH OUR
POWER, AND TEACH US,
THAT THE LESS WE
USE OUR POWER THE
GREATER IT WILL BE.

Thomas Jefferson

88

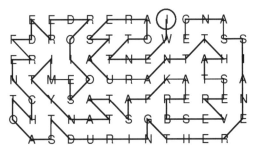

I WENT TO A
RESTAURANT THAT
SERVES "BREAKFAST AT
ANY TIME." SO I
ORDERED FRENCH
TOAST DURING THE
RENAISSANCE.

Steven Wright

89

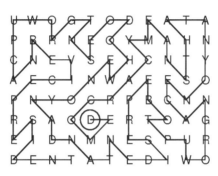

D E M O C R A C Y   M E A N S
T H A T   A N Y O N E   C A N
G R O W   U P   T O   B E
P R E S I D E N T,   A N D
A N Y O N E   W H O   D O E S N'T
G R O W   U P   C A N   B E   V I C E
P R E S I D E N T.

Johnny Carson

90

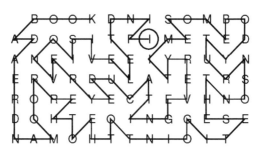

I FIND TELEVISION
VERY EDUCATING.
EVERY TIME SOMEBODY
TURNS ON THE SET, I
GO INTO THE OTHER
ROOM AND READ A
BOOK.

Groucho Marx

91

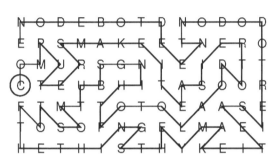

C O M P U T E R S   M A K E   I T
E A S I E R   T O   D O   A   L O T
O F   T H I N G S,   B U T   M O S T
O F   T H E   T H I N G S   T H E Y
M A K E   I T   E A S I E R   T O
D O   D O N'T   N E E D   T O   B E
D O N E.

Andy Rooney

92

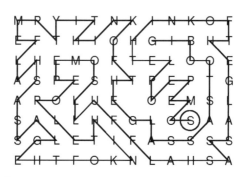

S O M E   P E O P L E   T H I N K
O F   T H E   G L A S S   A S
H A L F   F U L L.   S O M E
P E O P L E   T H I N K   O F   T H E
G L A S S   A S   H A L F   E M P T Y.
I   T H I N K   O F   T H E
G L A S S   A S   T O O   B I G.

George Carlin

93

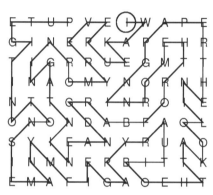

I WAKE UP EVERY
MORNING AT NINE AND
GRAB FOR THE
MORNING PAPER. THEN
I LOOK AT THE
OBITUARY PAGE. IF MY
NAME IS NOT ON IT, I
GET UP.

Benjamin Franklin

94

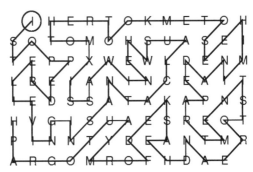

I STOPPED BELIEVING
IN SANTA CLAUS WHEN
I WAS SIX. MOTHER
TOOK ME TO SEE HIM
IN A DEPARTMENT
STORE AND HE ASKED
FOR MY AUTOGRAPH.

Shirley Temple

95

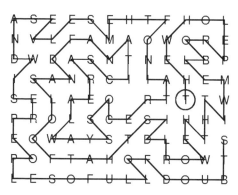

T H E   W H O L E   P R O B L E M
W I T H   T H E   W O R L D   I S
T H A T   F O O L S   A N D
F A N A T I C S   A R E   A L W A Y S
S O   C E R T A I N   O F
T H E M S E L V E S,   A N D
W I S E R   P E O P L E   S O
F U L L   O F   D O U B T S.

Bertrand Russell

96

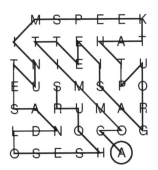

A   C O M M I T T E E   I S   A
G R O U P   T H A T   K E E P S
M I N U T E S   A N D   L O S E S
H O U R S.

Milton Berle

97

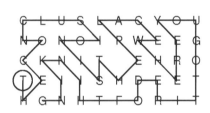

T H E   C O N C L U S I O N   I S
T H E   P L A C E   W H E R E   Y O U
G O T   T I R E D   O F
T H I N K I N G.

Arthur Bloch

98

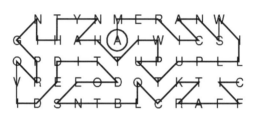

A M E R I C A N S   W I L L   P U T
U P   W I T H   A N Y T H I N G
P R O V I D E D   I T   D O E S N'T
B L O C K   T R A F F I C.

Dan Rather

99

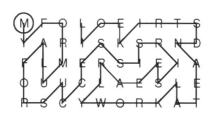

M Y   F O R M U L A   F O R
S U C C E S S   I S   R I S E
E A R L Y ,   W O R K   L A T E ,   A N D
S T R I K E   O I L .

Paul Getty

100

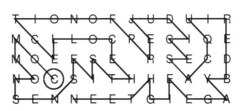

C O M M O N   S E N S E   I S   T H E

C O L L E C T I O N   O F

P R E J U D I C E S   A C Q U I R E D

B Y   A G E   E I G H T E E N.

Albert Einstein

101

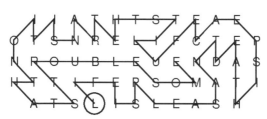

L I F E   I S   P L E A S A N T.
D E A T H   I S   P E A C E F U L.
I T'S   T H E   T R A N S I T I O N
T H A T'S   T R O U B L E S O M E.

Isaac Asimov

102

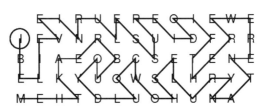

I BELIEVE IN RULES.
SURE I DO. IF THERE
WEREN'T ANY RULES,
HOW COULD YOU BREAK
THEM?

Leo Durocher

103

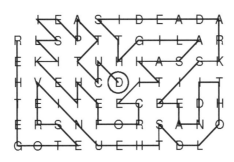

<u>D</u> <u>U</u> <u>C</u> <u>T</u>   <u>T</u> <u>A</u> <u>P</u> <u>E</u>   <u>I</u> <u>S</u>   <u>L</u> <u>I</u> <u>K</u> <u>E</u>
<u>T</u> <u>H</u> <u>E</u>   <u>F</u> <u>O</u> <u>R</u> <u>C</u> <u>E</u>.   <u>I</u> <u>T</u>   <u>H</u> <u>A</u> <u>S</u>   <u>A</u>
<u>L</u> <u>I</u> <u>G</u> <u>H</u> <u>T</u>   <u>S</u> <u>I</u> <u>D</u> <u>E</u>,   <u>A</u>   <u>D</u> <u>A</u> <u>R</u> <u>K</u>
<u>S</u> <u>I</u> <u>D</u> <u>E</u>,   <u>A</u> <u>N</u> <u>D</u>   <u>I</u> <u>T</u>   <u>H</u> <u>O</u> <u>L</u> <u>D</u> <u>S</u>
<u>T</u> <u>H</u> <u>E</u>   <u>U</u> <u>N</u> <u>I</u> <u>V</u> <u>E</u> <u>R</u> <u>S</u> <u>E</u>
<u>T</u> <u>O</u> <u>G</u> <u>E</u> <u>T</u> <u>H</u> <u>E</u> <u>R</u>.

Oprah Winfrey

104

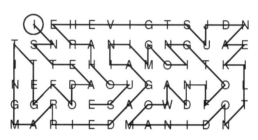

I N S T E A D   O F   G E T T I N G
M A R R I E D   A G A I N,   I ' M
G O I N G   T O   F I N D   A
W O M A N   I   D O N ' T   L I K E
A N D   J U S T   G I V E   H E R   A
H O U S E.

Rod Stewart

105

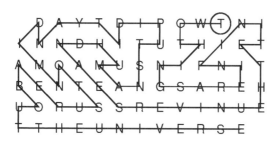

T W O   T H I N G S   A R E
I N F I N I T E   T H E
U N I V E R S E   A N D   H U M A N
S T U P I D I T Y;   A N D   I ' M
N O T   S U R E   A B O U T   T H E
U N I V E R S E.

Albert Einstein

106

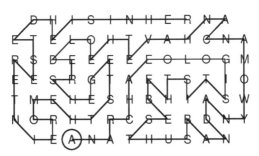

A N   A R C H A E O L O G I S T   I S
T H E   B E S T   H U S B A N D
A N Y   W O M A N   C A N   H A V E;
T H E   O L D E R   S H E   G E T S,
T H E   M O R E   I N T E R E S T E D
H E   I S   I N   H E R.

Agatha Christie

107

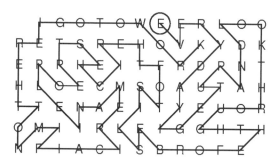

E V E R Y   D A Y   I   G E T   U P
A N D   L O O K   T H R O U G H
T H E   F O R B E S   L I S T   O F
T H E   R I C H E S T   P E O P L E
I N   A M E R I C A. I F   I'M
N O T   T H E R E, I   G O   T O
W O R K.

Robert Orben

108

243

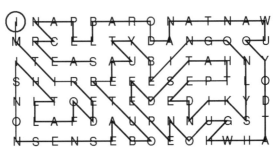

I'M TIRED OF ALL
THIS NONSENSE ABOUT
BEAUTY BEING ONLY
SKIN DEEP. THAT'S
DEEP ENOUGH. WHAT DO
YOU WANT? AN
ADORABLE PANCREAS?

Jean Kerr

109

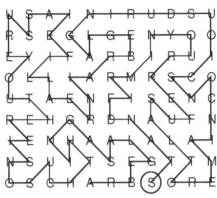

STAND FIRM IN YOUR
REFUSAL TO REMAIN
CONSCIOUS DURING
ALGEBRA. IN REAL
LIFE, I ASSURE YOU,
THERE IS NO SUCH
THING AS ALGEBRA.

Fran Lebowitz

110

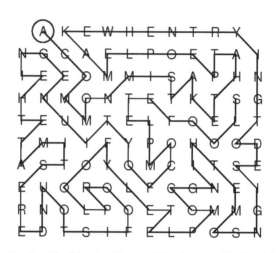

A COMMON MISTAKE
THAT PEOPLE MAKE
WHEN TRYING TO
DESIGN SOMETHING
COMPLETELY
FOOLPROOF IS TO
UNDERESTIMATE THE
INGENUITY OF
COMPLETE FOOLS.

Douglas Adams

111

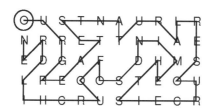

<u>O</u> <u>U</u> <u>R</u> <u>G</u> <u>R</u> <u>E</u> <u>A</u> <u>T</u> <u>E</u> <u>S</u> <u>T</u>
<u>N</u> <u>A</u> <u>T</u> <u>U</u> <u>R</u> <u>A</u> <u>L</u> <u>R</u> <u>E</u> <u>S</u> <u>O</u> <u>U</u> <u>R</u> <u>C</u> <u>E</u> <u>I</u> <u>S</u>
<u>T</u> <u>H</u> <u>E</u> <u>M</u> <u>I</u> <u>N</u> <u>D</u> <u>S</u> <u>O</u> <u>F</u> <u>O</u> <u>U</u> <u>R</u>
<u>C</u> <u>H</u> <u>I</u> <u>L</u> <u>D</u> <u>R</u> <u>E</u> <u>N</u>.

Walt Disney

112

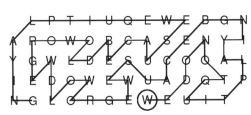

W E   D O   N O T   Q U I T
P L A Y I N G   B E C A U S E   W E
G R O W   O L D ,   W E   G R O W
O L D   B E C A U S E   W E   Q U I T
P L A Y I N G .

Oliver Wendell Holmes

113

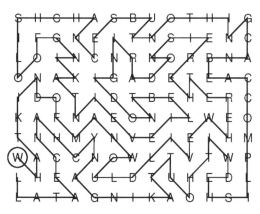

W H A T   K I N D   O F   M A N
W O U L D   L I V E   W H E R E
T H E R E   I S   N O   D A R I N G?
I   D O N'T   B E L I E V E   I N
T A K I N G   F O O L I S H
C H A N C E S,   B U T   N O T H I N G
C A N   B E   A C C O M P L I S H E D
W I T H O U T   T A K I N G   A N Y
C H A N C E   A T   A L L.

Charles Lindbergh

114

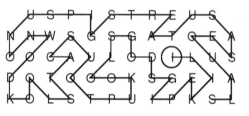

I LIKE PIGS. DOGS
LOOK UP TO US. CATS
LOOK DOWN ON US.
PIGS TREAT US AS
EQUALS.

Sir Winston Churchill

115

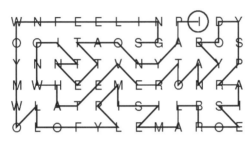

I PAY NO ATTENTION
WHATEVER TO
ANYBODY'S PRAISE OR
BLAME. I SIMPLY
FOLLOW MY OWN
FEELINGS.

Wolfgang Amadeus Mozart

116

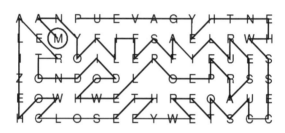

M A N Y   O F   L I F E'S
F A I L U R E S   A R E   P E O P L E
W H O   D I D   N O T   R E A L I Z E
H O W   C L O S E   T H E Y   W E R E
T O   S U C C E S S   W H E N
T H E Y   G A V E   U P.

Thomas A. Edison

117

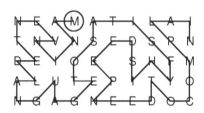

M A N   I N V E N T E D
L A N G U A G E   T O   S A T I S F Y
H I S   D E E P   N E E D   T O
C O M P L A I N.

Lily Tomlin

118

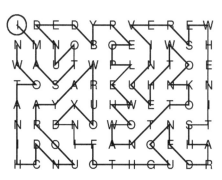

I'M ASTOUNDED BY
PEOPLE WHO WANT TO
"KNOW" THE UNIVERSE
WHEN IT'S HARD
ENOUGH TO FIND YOUR
WAY AROUND
CHINATOWN.

Woody Allen

119

Trickledowns:

Four-Letter Words:

1
PILL
POLL
POOL
POOR
DOOR

4
BAND
BIND
BINS
PINS
PIPS

2
SNOW
SLOW
SLAW
SLAY
PLAY

5
PULL
PILL
PILE
BILE
BITE

3
MOST
MOSS
MISS
HISS
HITS

6
DARE
DALE
BALE
BALD
BOLD

7

HYPE
HOPE
COPE
COPS
CONS

8

POST
PORT
PART
PARK
MARK

9

CASH
CAST
COST
LOST
LOOT

10

MICE
LICE
LIME
LAME
LAMB

11

COIN
CHIN
CHIP
SHIP
SHOP

12

DUDE
DUNE
DINE
MINE
MINT

13
MALT
MELT
BELT
BEET
BEER

14
PART
TART
TARS
TAPS
TIPS

15
LOST
LAST
LASS
MASS
MAPS

16
PINK
PINE
PILE
PALE
SALE

17
PEST
PAST
PASS
BASS
BATS

18
PAST
POST
POUT
POUR
FOUR

19
BACK
RACK
RACE
RICE
RIDE

22
TAKE
TAPE
TAPS
TIPS
RIPS

20
WAND
WANT
RANT
RUNT
RUST

23
MARE
MORE
MODE
NODE
NODS

21
CARE
DARE
DIRE
DIRT
DIET

24
MOOD
MOON
MORN
TORN
TURN

25
TORT
TART
TARS
TAGS
BAGS

26
MEAN
MOAN
MORN
WORN
WORM

27
MOVE
COVE
CORE
CARE
CARS

28
POPS
PUPS
CUPS
CUTS
CUTE

29
BELT
BELL
DELL
DULL
DUEL

30
BALD
BALE
TALE
TILE
TIRE

31

BAND
BOND
BONE
BORE
LORE

32

PARK
PERK
PERT
PEST
REST

33

HARD
HARE
HIRE
HIVE
DIVE

34

FEAR
BEAR
BEAD
BEND
BOND

35

TOOK
ROOK
ROCK
RACK
RACE

36

LAME
LIME
LINE
LINT
PINT

37
HATE
HATS
HITS
HISS
KISS

38
ZANY
MANY
MANE
MINE
MICE

39
FAST
FIST
MIST
MINT
MIND

40
FLAW
FLOW
SLOW
SLOT
SPOT

41
SWIM
SLIM
SLUM
PLUM
PLUG

42
CATS
CANS
CANE
CONE
NONE

43
BALL
BILL
FILL
FILE
FIRE

44
MEAL
MEAT
MOAT
MOST
HOST

45
FIST
GIST
GILT
GILL
GALL

46
GRAM
CRAM
CLAM
CLAD
CLOD

47
TOWN
TORN
TORE
TARE
BARE

48
MATH
BATH
BATS
BAYS
BOYS

49
PLUG
SLUG
SLAG
STAG
STAY

50
VOTE
TOTE
TOTS
TOPS
TIPS

51
LAME
SAME
SOME
SORE
SORT

52
LEGS
PEGS
PIGS
PINS
PINE

53
MOTH
BOTH
BATH
BATE
BANE

54
VASE
CASE
CARE
CORE
CORD

55
MESS
LESS
LOSS
LOST
LOOT

56
FIND
MIND
MINE
MANE
MARE

57
PEAS
SEAS
SEAL
SELL
SILL

58
CAST
CASE
BASE
BANE
BONE

59
CAMP
CAME
SAME
SATE
SITE

60
FACT
PACT
PACE
PARE
PURE

61
FOLD
BOLD
BALD
BALE
BARE

62
TONE
LONE
LANE
LAND
LAUD

63
BILL
MILL
MALL
MALE
MANE

64
GAME
SAME
SANE
SANG
SONG

65
HITS
BITS
BATS
BARS
BARD

66
LIST
MIST
MISS
MASS
MAPS

67
TACT
PACT
PACE
PALE
POLE

68
DARE
DART
TART
TORT
TOUT

69
WISP
WISE
RISE
ROSE
ROPE

70
SEED
REED
READ
ROAD
ROAM

71
FORM
FORD
WORD
WARD
WAND

72
WISH
WASH
WASP
HASP
HARP

73
BIND
BIRD
BARD
BARN
DARN

74
LAME
LANE
LONE
LONG
SONG

75
ZOOM
ZOOS
MOOS
MOMS
MUMS

76
HOOT
HOOP
COOP
CORP
CARP

77
MASK
MAST
CAST
COST
COLT

78
PALL
PALS
PATS
CATS
CUTS

79
FOOD
FOOL
FOIL
SOIL
SAIL

82
MILK
MILD
MOLD
FOLD
FOND

80
JACK
RACK
ROCK
ROOK
ROOM

83
DIME
TIME
TILE
TILL
TOLL

81
TYPE
TAPE
CAPE
CAPS
CARS

84
PINT
PUNT
PUNS
GUNS
GUTS

85
WARS
WART
MART
MALT
MOLT

86
YULE
MULE
MALE
MARE
MART

87
DIME
RIME
RITE
ROTE
ROTS

88
DIME
DIMS
RIMS
RAMS
RAYS

89
PALM
PALL
FALL
FAIL
FOIL

90
MIST
MOST
COST
COAT
COAL

91
NEST
PEST
PAST
PACT
PACE

92
MAKE
MARE
WARE
WORE
WORD

93
DIME
DAME
DALE
MALE
MALT

94
PALM
BALM
BALE
BILE
BITE

95
WANT
WART
WARM
WORM
FORM

96
NEST
BEST
BUST
BUNT
BUNS

97
BOOM
ROOM
ROAM
ROAD
READ

98
TARP
TARE
BARE
BORE
BONE

99
RACE
FACE
FACT
FAST
FIST

100
BOOM
BOON
BORN
BURN
TURN

101
LAWN
DAWN
DARN
DARE
DIRE

102
HEEL
HEED
SEED
SHED
SHOD

103
CROW
CREW
BREW
BLEW
BLED

104
COAT
COST
CAST
CASE
VASE

105
BEST
WEST
WELT
WELL
WILL

106
FOUL
FOOL
COOL
COOT
CLOT

107
HUNT
BUNT
BUST
BUSH
BASH

108
JUMP
DUMP
DAMP
DAME
DARE

109
CLOD
CLOT
SLOT
SLIT
SKIT

110
BOAT
BOAS
BIAS
BIBS
DIBS

111
FOAL
FOIL
FAIL
FAIR
HAIR

112
CLIP
SLIP
SHIP
SHOP
SHOD

113
POOL
COOL
COAL
COAT
CHAT

114
FOOT
FORT
TORT
TART
TARP

115
PEEL
REEL
REED
READ
ROAD

116
RACE
PACE
PACT
PANT
PINT

117
TOOL
TOLL
ROLL
ROLE
RULE

118
PUPS
CUPS
COPS
CONS
CONE

119
BURP
BUMP
BUMS
GUMS
GEMS

120
SIFT
RIFT
RAFT
RANT
RANK

121
PORT
PORE
PARE
CARE
CAPE

122
PELT
MELT
MALT
MALL
MAIL

Five-Letter Words:

123
CHOPS
SHOPS
SLOPS
SLOTS
SLATS
SLATE

124
SCARE
SCALE
SHALE
SHALL
SHILL
CHILL

125
FLEET
SLEET
SLEEP
STEEP
STREP
STRIP

126
CRUSH
CRASH
CLASH
CLASS
CLAMS
SLAMS

127
GOODY
GOODS
MOODS
MOLDS
MOLES
MILES

128
CREST
CHEST
CHESS
CHEWS
CHOWS
SHOWS

129
BROWN
CROWN
CROWS
CROPS
CHOPS
CHIPS

130
MISTY
MUSTY
MUSTS
RUSTS
RUNTS
RUNGS

131
TAPED
TAPES
CAPES
COPES
CORES
CORNS

132
BLOWN
BLOWS
BLOBS
BLABS
SLABS
STABS

133
THANK
SHANK
SPANK
SPARK
SPARE
SPIRE

136
STARE
SHARE
SHORE
SHONE
PHONE
PHONY

134
SLANG
SLING
SWING
SWINE
TWINE
TWICE

137
CRASH
CLASH
CLASS
CLAMS
SLAMS
SLUMS

135
GLOOM
BLOOM
BROOM
BROOD
BROAD
BREAD

138
GRASP
GRASS
GLASS
CLASS
CLAPS
CLIPS

139
THING
THINK
THICK
CHICK
CLICK
CLUCK

142
CROWN
CROWS
CROPS
CHOPS
CHIPS
SHIPS

140
CRUSH
CRASH
CLASH
CLASS
CLAPS
SLAPS

143
CLICK
SLICK
SLICE
SPICE
SPIRE
SPARE

141
CLOCK
CLICK
SLICK
SLICE
SPICE
SPIRE

144
TWICE
TWINE
SWINE
SPINE
SPINS
SPANS

145
CRAMP
CRIMP
CRIME
CLIME
SLIME
SLICE

146
PARTY
PARTS
PORTS
TORTS
TOOTS
TOOLS

147
PENCE
PEACE
PLACE
PLANE
PLANT
SLANT

148
TRAIN
BRAIN
BRAID
BRAND
BLAND
BLOND

149
PATHS
PATES
MATES
MITES
MITER
MISER

150
SHORT
SHORE
SHONE
PHONE
PRONE
PRUNE

151
SLOPE
SLOPS
SHOPS
SHIPS
SHIMS
WHIMS

152
WOODY
WORDY
WORDS
WORMS
FORMS
FARMS

153
TRACK
TRICK
TRICE
TWICE
TWINE
SWINE

154
TRACK
TRACE
TRADE
GRADE
GLADE
GLIDE

155
TRUCK
TRACK
TRACE
TRADE
GRADE
GLADE

156
TWICE
TWINE
SWINE
SWING
STING
STUNG

157
BLOCK
BLACK
SLACK
STACK
STARK
START

158
CHORD
CHORE
SHORE
STORE
STARE
STAGE

159
SCENT
SCANT
SLANT
PLANT
PLANE
PLATE

160
STONE
SHONE
SHINE
SHINS
CHINS
CHIPS

161
COINS
CORNS
CORES
CARES
DARES
DARED

162
MOODY
MOODS
MOLDS
MOLES
ROLES
RULES

163
TILED
TIRED
SIRED
SIRES
SORES
SORTS

164
SHOOT
SHOOK
SHOCK
CHOCK
CLOCK
CLICK

165
CRACK
CRANK
CLANK
CLANG
SLANG
SLING

166
FINED
FINES
DINES
DUNES
DUNKS
DUCKS

167
DROWN
BROWN
BLOWN
BLOWS
BLOBS
BLABS

168
ATONE
STONE
SHONE
SHORE
SHORT
SHIRT

169
THINK
THANK
SHANK
SHARK
STARK
START

170
SCALE
SCARE
SCORE
SHORE
CHORE
CHORD

171
PARTY
PARTS
PANTS
PINTS
PINES
DINES

172
SHAME
SHARE
SCARE
SCORE
SCORN
ACORN

173
PHONE
SHONE
SCONE
SCORE
SCARE
SCARF

174
CLASP
CLASS
GLASS
GRASS
GROSS
GROWS

175
BLOWS
GLOWS
GROWS
GROSS
GRASS
GRASP

176
MINOR
MINER
DINER
DINES
DUNES
DUDES

177
BELLY
BELLS
TELLS
TOLLS
TOOLS
TOOTS

178
FLUSH
BLUSH
BRUSH
BRASH
BRASS
BRATS

179
GRAND
BRAND
BLAND
BLEND
BLEED
BLEEP

180
CROWD
CROWS
CROSS
GROSS
GRASS
GLASS

181
CHILL
SHILL
SHALL
STALL
STALE
STARE

182
STUNT
STINT
SAINT
PAINT
PAINS
PAIRS

183
CHIMP
CHAMP
CLAMP
CLAMS
SLAMS
SLAPS

184
STORM
STORE
SHORE
CHORE
CHOSE
CHASE

Six-Letter Words:

185
PASTOR
PASTER
PASTED
POSTED
HOSTED
HOOTED
HOOKED

186
GLAZED
GRAZED
GRACED
TRACED
TRACES
TRACKS
TRUCKS

187
PLANET
PLANES
PLANKS
CLANKS
CRANKS
CRACKS
CROCKS

188
SLICES
SLICKS
CLICKS
CRICKS
CRACKS
CRANKS
CRANKY

189
TRADED
TRACED
TRACES
TRACKS
CRACKS
CROCKS
CLOCKS

190
THINKS
THANKS
SHANKS
SPANKS
SPARKS
SPARES
SPARED

191
TRICKY
TRICKS
TRACKS
CRACKS
CRANKS
CLANKS
CLANGS

192
TAILOR
TAILER
TAILED
FAILED
FOILED
FOOLED
FOOTED

193
THANKS
SHANKS
SPANKS
SPARKS
SPARES
SPIRES
SPIRED

194
TOOTED
TOOLED
TOILED
SOILED
SAILED
SAILER
SAILOR

195
LASSOS
LASSES
PASSES
PARSES
PURSES
PURGES
PURGED

196
PASTOR
PASTER
PASTED
POSTED
POUTED
POURED
TOURED

Acknowledgments

This book would not have been possible without the work and suggestions of the following people: Mr. Anthony Immanuvel of Yoogi Games (www.yoogi.com), Ms. Brooke Dworkin, Ms. Megan Rotondo, and Ms. Karen Backstein. Finally, I would like to say a special thank-you to my right hand and the person who makes all this happen, Mrs. Christy Davis, owner of Executive Services in Arlington, Texas.